MORE PRAISE FOR *GENEROSITY WINS*

"The authors of *Generosity Wins* have honed in on the concept of generosity as a tool, as a vehicle, but, quite rightly, highlight and embody it as one of the things that is core to what makes us human. Wood and Roberts challenge the reader to question, apply, and then master this concept of generosity as a new superpower. Readers are challenged to explore and question their own generosity. The result is a powerful paradigm shift in how we see ourselves and others through a new lens of giving."

— **Marc Ó Gríofa**, MD PhD FAWM FEWM FFSEM, medical director, CMO/CTO, Explorer's Club fellow

"I've written about the significance and power of generosity many times, and now we have a terrific book that helps redefine and make it accessible for everyone!"

— **Rishad Tobaccowala**, author of *Restoring the Soul of Business: Staying Human in the Age of Data*, advisor, speaker, and educator

"*Generosity Wins* is a wonderful book! I grew up with the saying, 'If you want to be happy, think what you can do for someone else,' and to my mind, *Generosity Wins* will provide you with the keys to happiness."

— **Mitzi Perdue (Mrs. Frank Perdue)**, author and anti-human trafficking advocate

"Giving with passion is powerful, but *Generosity Wins* brings it to life. I encourage everyone to read this book and put the power to use."

— **Cosmo DeNicola**, chairman of DeNicola Family Foundation

"After reading *Generosity Wins*, I realized that humility, kindness, and generosity are interconnected. This book gives you excellent knowledge, science, and understanding, but more importantly, it provides tools for success that you can deploy immediately and every day."

— **Sarfaraz K. Niazi**, PhD, adjunct professor, University of Illinois

"If you're ready to awaken the hidden giant of generosity deep within you, read this important book and leverage your success and happiness exponentially."

— **Jim Karol**, memory edutainer

"Superpower is a big concept, but *Generosity Wins* brings it to life. Technology acts as an accelerator for nearly everything in our lives, including the impact of generosity. This book is a must-read to harness your superpower."

> **- David Clarke**, digital entrepreneur, investor, former PWC global chief experience officer, and BGT chief executive officer

"I've always subscribed to the notion that kindness and generosity play a huge part in personal success and fulfillment. Wood and Roberts validate this in *Generosity Wins*. This book serves as a guide, a reminder, and a great asset on becoming a better leader and person."

> **- Rodney Clark**, vice president and chief commercial officer of Johnson Controls

"The secret to success is not in how much you gain but in how much you give. This insightful book looks at how the free gift of generosity can level the playing field of success."

> **- Melissa Dawn Simkins**, CEO of Velvet Suite and founder of The She-Suite

"Wood and Roberts share with the world what we should all know: the way to happiness is generosity. Until you serve others, joy is impossible."

> **- Sara O'Meara**, cofounder, chairman, and CEO of ChildHelp

"Generosity is required for any of life's relationships to be happy and functional. You need to be generous with your time, generous with your things, and generous with your praise to make a true difference in the life of someone else. Bravo on this important book!"

> **- Crystal Dwyer Hansen**, international success coach and bestselling author of *ASK! The Bridge from Your Dreams to Your Destiny*

"*Generosity Wins* is the reminder we all need that we work better when we look out for each other."

> **- Jess Ekstrom**, author of *Chasing the Bright Side*

"*Generosity Wins* should be required reading for all as it reminds us that the true art of hospitality is not transactional but starts with a superpower everyone can master—generosity!"

> **- Michael Dominguez**, president and CEO of Associated Luxury Hotels International

MONTE WOOD
NICOLE F. ROBERTS, DrPH

GENEROSITY
WINS

HOW AND WHY THIS
GAME-CHANGING SUPERPOWER
DRIVES OUR SUCCESS

Generosity Wins: How and Why This Game-Changing Superpower Drives Our Success

Copyright © 2023 by Monte Wood and Nicole F. Roberts

Published by Worth Books, an imprint of Forefront Books.
Distributed by Simon & Schuster.

Library of Congress Control Number: 2023914459

Print ISBN: 978-1-63763-181-2
E-book ISBN: 978-1-63763-182-9

Cover Design by George Stevens
Interior Design by Bill Kersey, KerseyGraphics

We dedicate this book to those who have

blessed and inspired us with generosity.

We are but limbs on the trees you planted.

TABLE OF CONTENTS

To the Reader:

As you embark on this adventure with us, please know that we are profoundly grateful for, and inspired by, the individuals whose expertise, insights, and practical wisdom you will encounter in the following pages. While our main character, Emily, is fictitious, the highly accomplished people she interviews along her journey, and the words they share, are very real indeed. Follow the QR link at the end of each chapter to learn more about the individual.

These interviews combined with extensive research into the science and studies on the subject, prompted us to radically redefine and reposition generosity. We have made the power of generosity available to anyone, and everyone, at any stage of life. Read on to learn exactly why generosity is a superpower for personal success.

*

GENEROSITY:
Any act of kindness or support, given with no expectation of exchange or return from the recipient(s). There are limitless meaningful ways to be generous.

*

HUMAN GENEROSITY:
Humans are the only species known to be generous with others they aren't associated with, don't know, or may never know. This unique attribute is credited to perpetuating the evolution of our civilization.

*

GENEROSITY ROI:

*Invest in being generous every day and expect great things
to happen. Benefiting yourself by being generous with
others, with no expectation of exchange or return from the
recipient(s), is how and why generosity is a superpower.*

*

SELF-GENEROSITY:

*Any action one takes that moves them closer
to becoming the person they aspire to be.
Overindulgence is not self-generosity.*

*

SUCCESS:

*Success is the ideal combination of
passion, joy, and accomplishment.
The ideal combination of each is different for everyone,
but comprehensive success requires all three.*

*

EUDEMONIC SUCCESS:

*The type of happiness, contentment, or success that
is achieved through self-actualization and having
meaningful purpose in one's life.
Generosity fuels Eudemonic Success.*

CHAPTER 1

A JOLTING CONFRONTATION

In the entire history of the hospitality industry, no general manager of a luxury property had ever gone into her semi-annual review with higher expectations and hopes.

Emily Gardner, six months shy of her thirtieth birthday, had enjoyed a spectacularly rapid ascent through the ranks at Pinafore Global, one of the world's leading hotel chains. After graduating from Cornell University's School of Hotel Administration at age twenty-two, she had taken on increasingly important roles at Pinafore properties in Istanbul, Hong Kong, Brussels, and most recently San Diego.

On her watch, the numbers for the San Diego property were pretty impressive—costs were down, average room rates were up. Okay, occupancy was flat and there were a handful, or maybe more than a handful, of negative reviews on Tripadvisor, which had never happened to that property before. *But what are you going to do?* Emily told herself as she headed into her CEO's office. *You can't please everyone all the time, right?*

So it was all the more shocking and deflating when Emily entered the LA office of her mentor—Don Jenkins—saw the look on his face, and read his body language. Don, recently promoted to CEO of Pinafore, was a forty-seven-year-old executive who was now responsible for all dimensions of success for a very highly respected global company.

Don was a tall, handsome African American executive who had come to Pinafore ten years ago, having worked at three other international hospitality groups. He had hired Emily out of Cornell after meeting her on the campus of his alma mater during a speaking engagement. He saw a bit of himself in this confident redhead and had quietly mentored her from her earliest days at the company. He was also influential in bringing her home from Europe and giving her the top job at the San Diego property, a decision that took a lot of diplomacy to get through the executive team. Don's colleagues thought Emily too young and unseasoned for the role. Don had believed otherwise.

Emily could read a room. She immediately saw that Don looked more like an executioner than the bearer of good news.

"What's wrong?" Emily asked, suddenly on edge.

Emily had always assumed that having Don as a mentor would have a slingshot effect on her career. Maybe now, though, the opposite was true. Don stood up from behind his desk and sat opposite her on the couch in his large office.

"You aren't getting it done," Don said, his expression grim, getting right to the point. "We have to relieve you of your duties in San Diego."

Emily felt as if she had been punched in the gut.

"But...why?" she asked, mystified. "Revenue's up, costs are down... what did I do wrong? Is this some sort of political thing?"

"It's got nothing to do with politics," Don said, shaking his head sadly, his intense eyes boring into Emily's. "It's just the way you've been doing things."

"I thought I was nailing it!" she exclaimed. "You saw my reviews in Hong Kong. In Istanbul. Everywhere. What do you mean, the way I've been doing things?"

Don leaned forward and tapped a file folder on the table between them.

"It's all in here," he said. "I'm going to ask you to read this after our meeting is over. But I will bottom-line it for you."

Emily was blinking back tears. The last thing she wanted to do was cry in front of the CEO. That would be humiliating.

"You are a good professional," Don said, and the warmth in his tone took some of the sting out of his words. "No one questions your abilities as a manager. And everybody is aware of the results you have gotten. It is just a question of exactly what results and *how* those results have been achieved."

"So what exactly am I doing that is so wrong?" Emily said, shaking her head. "Look at the numbers!"

Don put a hand up.

"Emily," he began, "in every industry, not just hospitality, there's more to it than just the numbers." He sighed. "We both know that. This is the first time you have been in charge of a property. And the way you've been doing things is not the Pinafore way."

"Could I please get a for-instance?" Emily asked, still confused.

"You let go three of the long-term loyal housekeepers," Don began.

"They were underperforming," Emily countered. "There were complaints. You're firing me because I let go some housekeepers who didn't live up to our standards?"

"You didn't hire new ones," Don said. "Instead, you gave their workload to the ones who were remaining. All of this without explanation and counter to what your managers recommended."

"And that is a fireable offense?" Emily asked, feeling as if she had entered some sort of bizarro world. "It's a standard cost-cutting move. Everybody does it."

"That's not true," Don said in a soft voice, but his gentle tone hardly cushioned the blow Emily was experiencing. "Lots of companies avoid cutting loyal team members and dumping work onto the people who haven't been fired. It's not universal. And it's certainly not how *we* operate. Did they ever do that at any of the properties you worked at in Europe?"

Emily sighed. She knew the answer was no.

"You got rid of the turndown service," Don continued, referring to the practice of turning down the sheets and blankets on guests' beds in the evening.

"Do you realize what that costs in overtime?" Emily asked, her tone indignant. "That was a significant cost savings for the company. I think I should be thanked for that!"

"You also cut back on the concierge staff by 40 percent," Don said. "Now there's nobody at the concierge desk between midnight and 6:00 a.m."

"We're talking about *San Diego!*" Emily replied with dismay. "How many people need concierge service between midnight and 6:00 a.m.?"

"We are a seven-star property," Don said. "Only if it is one or two a night, we still offer it. I could go on, but I think you get the drift."

"I get the drift all right," Emily said, deeply unhappy now. "I'm being fired because of some cost-cutting moves that we both know helped the bottom line."

Don continued, "Your costs are down and your profit is up slightly, but the market has grown over the last year and your occupancy is flat. This is not a good indicator of where the business will go in the future. You know that.

"The bottom line isn't the only measure of success," Don added. "There are other key 'metrics,' if you will. Not just in business but in life.

One of the most important is a spirit of generosity. Do you remember that time in Hong Kong when a guest from Mongolia left his winter coat at the hotel, and you arranged for a courier to send it back to him in Ulan Bator, where it was ten below zero that week?"

> **"The bottom line isn't the only measure of success."**

"Of course," she said, thinking back. "I got a commendation for that."

"And do you remember the time," Don continued, "in Istanbul, a family went to the wrong port for their cruise ship when they left the hotel?"

"It happens all the time," Emily said, rolling her eyes. "Istanbul can be really confusing. There are two areas where cruise ships leave from. No matter how often we tell the guests..."

"You hired a helicopter to get them to the next port on the cruise," Don recalled.

"The husband had cancer," Emily said, nodding. "He was a history buff and he had never seen the Dardanelles. What was I supposed to do—let him miss his cruise?"

"Exactly," Don replied. "*That* is how Pinafore does things. But once you got your own property, it's like the whole generosity focus went out the window."

"San Diego was underperforming for years before I got there," Emily said hotly. "That's why you sent me there. To turn it around. How am I supposed to do that without cutting costs?"

"My *expectation*," Don said, choosing his words carefully, "was that the same spirit of generosity that motivated you to send that coat and hire that helicopter would be your guiding principle in growing San Diego."

"You are telling me that I should have spent money willy-nilly," Emily said, stung. "*That's* how a distressed hotel gets back on its feet?"

"I'm not saying you should have spent willy-nilly," Don said gently. "I am saying that you weren't building a sound foundation. *Inconsistent* is the best way to describe things. You had good quarters and not-so-good quarters. You got rave reviews and bad reviews. Your growth trended behind in a strong market. Your team was disenchanted with your hardcore ways and lack of collaboration. They felt like you didn't care about anything but profit. We build success with a focus on brand loyalty, a tenured team, long-term results, and consistency. Does that make sense?"

"I'm really confused," Emily said, raising a hand to her temple. "I should have hired more helicopters? Spent more money? Is that it?"

"What we look for," Don explained gently, "is growth matched by leading with important values, specifically, generosity and caring. That's the Pinafore way."

"That's what I was trying to do," Emily said, feeling her whole world crashing at her feet.

"Let me ask a completely different question," Don said, studying Emily carefully. "You getting enough sleep?"

"That's kind of personal," Emily said defensively, thinking the question completely out of left field but strangely pertinent. Then she dropped her guard. "Actually...no. I'm not. I feel like I'm always worried and working around the clock."

Don nodded empathetically and got back to his main point.

"The three examples I gave," Don said, not wanting to pile on, but needing to make the point, "are representative of the way things were done on your watch at San Diego. In that file you will find two dozen more. Look, I think you have a bright future with this company."

"But you're firing me!" Emily exclaimed, now thoroughly confused. "How could I have a bright future?"

"You are *not* being fired," Don said. "Your salary is going to remain the same. Your benefits are untouched. It is just that I can't have you running San Diego the way you have been running it."

"Give me another chance," Emily said quickly, almost pleading with him. "I hear what you are saying. I can do things differently. I can hire some more concierges and cleaning staff. I'll work on collaborating better and improving the customer reviews. Please don't do this to me."

Don shook his head.

"No can do," he said. "Look, you've got the right instincts. But there is more that you need to learn about our values and why they are so important. Both professionally and personally. We are at the high end of the high end when it comes to what people pay to stay with us. There are high expectations. I need you to have a clear understanding of exactly how we meet those expectations. Which is why I have a different assignment for you."

"What kind of assignment?" Emily asked, studying him.

"It's also in here," Don said, gently pushing the folder across the table to Emily. "Take it with you, get a cup of coffee, take a deep breath, and then read everything. And if you are open to it, let me know. But I need to know within forty-eight hours."

"Are you demoting me?" Emily asked, still bewildered. "Is that it? Or are you basically having me fire myself?"

Don laughed, which surprised Emily even more.

"Far from it," he said. "*I believe in you.* But you've veered down a wrong path. I need to see something different from you, and that is only going to happen if you learn more about what differentiates us and facilitates our consistent success. It's all about success, in a broad sense, not just in financial terms, and how to attract it year after year. Just take the folder. And call me. But within forty-eight hours. I need an answer."

Don stood, indicating that the meeting was over. Emily rose, reached forward, and took the folder, wondering what on earth was in it and what on earth Don expected her to do.

"I'm sorry I let you down," she said meekly.

"In some places," Don said, "they might reward you for what you did and how you did it. But great companies don't run that way. Pinafore certainly doesn't. You've worked here for years. You should know that better than anyone. Take a look at the assignment. Let me know."

Emily looked up at him, sighed, and said, "Okay," because there was nothing else to say.

Still reeling but curious about what Don had in mind, she headed out of the office.

CHAPTER 2

CHALLENGE ACCEPTED

Emily, still in shock, got into her rental car and found a Starbucks a mile and a half from Pinafore's headquarters. The last thing she wanted to do was to run into colleagues at a coffee shop nearby and have to describe what had just happened.

She parked, headed inside, ordered a latte, then sat down at a table in the mostly empty coffee shop. After all, it was still the workday, and suddenly she realized how lucky she was to still have a job. All for doing, as Don even said, what could have gotten her a promotion at another company.

She opened the folder and began to read. The first document was a list of changes she had instituted at the San Diego Pinafore property. She scanned the list and remembered each of the decisions she had made. Were they solely her decisions and counter to what her managers recommended? Yep. Had quality been compromised? Perhaps. Could she have been a little more thoughtful in giving people guidance and second chances? Maybe. But the numbers spoke for themselves. Even with flat bookings, she had brought San Diego into the black. Was what she had done really so wrong?

She put the memo aside and turned to Don's letter.

Emily,

Generosity is a much more complex behavior than people think, and generosity is core to both the company's mission and my personal values. Many people confuse generosity with altruism or financial philanthropy. Altruism is essentially giving oneself up to benefit another. Financial philanthropy is primarily just giving money. With true generosity, however, everyone benefits—the giver *and* the receiver, and all those around them. You could spend a lifetime studying the principles of generosity. I don't pretend to know everything about it, but on the other hand, I know people who know a lot.

I am therefore going to ask you to spend the next six months traveling around the United States and meeting with some of the country's most successful leaders, educators, artists, scientists, and overall wise people whom I've gotten to know over the course of my career. They are family friends, guests at Pinafore properties, investors, consultants, and many of whom I admittedly think of as close friends. They are a remarkable group of individuals.

I want you to meet with each of them, learn their stories, hear their words, see where they came from, see what they have achieved, and see how generosity has been the driving force in their lives and in their success.

> **"The same way people often don't understand generosity, they often misunderstand success too."**

Are these individuals ambitious? Absolutely. When we think of ambition, sometimes we think in terms of selfishness. These are individuals who wanted to create success for themselves. At the same time, they wanted to create success for thousands or even millions of others. And that is exactly what they have done in their personal and professional lives as well as their communities. The ripple effect of their generosity will likely astound you.

The same way people often don't understand generosity, they often misunderstand success too. When we speak about "successful" people, we usually think in very narrow terms. Often just career or financial net worth. Success is actually much broader. A truly successful person succeeds not just at the office and financially but also in his or her marriage, family, emotional life, spiritual life, and physical well-being. One can't be optimally generous with others unless they have effectively defined their vision and cared for themselves. The individuals you will meet have created success in most or all of these areas. They have learned how to use generosity with others and themselves. The combination is extremely powerful.

I'm proposing a six-month assignment, in which at the end I want you to come back to my office and tell me what you have learned. I want a full report.

My hope is that you will return with an entirely different view of generosity and success. Those actions you took in Hong Kong, Istanbul, and at other moments in your career suggest that you are the right person to undertake this mission.

The Pinafore executive team has decided to create a new senior role in the company, the CGO, Chief Generosity Officer. If things proceed in a way that makes sense for you and the organization, we would move you to this important new position. We would then ask you to share your knowledge by doing presentations and training on our values at our various properties on the six continents we serve. I know you love to travel; I'm hoping you find this opportunity attractive.

I would not be able to give you any meaningful position in the company if you turn this mission down. I will write you a stellar letter of recommendation, and I will call colleagues at other enterprises that might welcome someone who can cut costs, streamline, and so on. And you'll do fine in any of those places.

But I don't think that is who you are. I don't think that is what you stand for or what you really want.

I know it sounds a little weird. Talking to people and then taking on a role essentially advocating for strong values and generosity company-wide. But I think you are the perfect person to do this, and quite frankly, I think it is going to be a heck of a lot of fun.

I need to know within forty-eight hours what your decision will be.

I'm hoping you will say yes.

Sincerely, Don.

> "With true generosity, everyone benefits—the giver *and* the receiver, and all those around them."

Emily read the letter a second time, still wondering if she was dreaming and if she would wake up and realize that her interview with Don was still a few hours away. No such luck. This was real. This was happening. She had lost her position running the San Diego property, doing exactly what she thought she needed to do.

On the other hand, the idea of meeting these high-level individuals and learning more about their journeys...it sounded kind of cool. Something different. It was just six months, in any event, and concluded about the same time as a reflective, milestone birthday. She had been struggling a bit personally and had broken up with her boyfriend a few months earlier. They had both been working at the Pinafore property in Istanbul, and he was now working at their hotel in Paris. The long distance between them had made the relationship difficult, at least for her. There was really nothing tying her to one place. So what if she lived out of airports and hotels for a while? She always liked hotels from the time she was a little kid. That is why she went into hospitality in the first place.

And the idea of getting back to what Don called the "spirit of generosity" appealed to her. It felt natural, authentic, true to who she really was, true to who she wanted to be. In a way, it was a relief to give up the hardball mentality, all the worry about the bottom line, and the anxiety caused by that increasing drumbeat of negative reviews.

What the heck, she thought. Chief Generosity Officer? Was Pinafore really going to pay for such a thing? Well, Don said so, and he had never lied to her.

Emily sipped her latte, thought for a long moment, took a deep breath, and exhaled.

She reached for her phone and texted Don.

"I'm in."

CHAPTER 3

THE ENVELOPE, PLEASE

The next three days for Emily went by in a painful blur as she cleared out the office she loved at the property she loved, and had to say goodbye to her staff. Many assumed that she was being promoted, but she was sure some of them suspected otherwise. She was hardly about to tell them that Pinafore Global was giving her an insane assignment, likely inviting her to quit so that they wouldn't have to fire her. She simply kept mum when people asked what her next assignment would be, explaining that corporate was still deciding where to send her. That satisfied all her reports, but it certainly didn't satisfy her.

Don texted Emily and asked her to meet at the property that afternoon, the third day since their fateful conversation in his office. He was in town and suggested they meet on the veranda of the hotel, overlooking Mission Bay. It was the very spot where Emily had enjoyed a latte and a croissant every morning as she planned her working day. It was heartbreaking for her to make that the scene of her final farewell to the San

Diego Pinafore, but if that is where Don wanted to meet, then that was the plan.

Don was famous for getting to meetings fifteen minutes before they were to start. Emily had known this trait of her boss for many years, found it very respectful, and decided that she would arrive at the same time he did. And that is why both Don and Emily were approaching the veranda from different directions fifteen minutes early.

Don, like Emily, had the ability to read a room, or in this case, a veranda.

"You don't look happy," Don observed, as he settled into an elegant deck chair and signaled for the server to approach.

"How could I be?" Emily asked, trying to keep her composure. She had promised herself that she would not get emotional in this conversation, no matter how upset she felt. She loved the San Diego Pinafore, she loved the role, and she loved the veranda. Giving it all up was deeply painful, especially for something so obscure as Don's plan for her.

"I understand how you feel," Don said empathetically. "I get it."

"What I get," Emily said, her eyes staring into his, "is that you have created this nonsensical task so that I will get bored, give up, and quit. That way, the company won't have to fire me or get sued."

"Utterly incorrect," Don said firmly and a bit frustrated. And to the server: "Two lattes and two croissants." He glanced back at Emily. "That is what you like, isn't it?"

Emily nodded and exhaled deeply. He knew everything about her, including what she ordered at the property every morning. He had an easy way of making her feel special.

The server went off to place the order.

Don leaned forward.

"You are not, repeat *not* being fired," Don said emphatically. "Do not underestimate the importance of what I'm asking you to do. It is so much bigger than running a hotel. It may not feel that way today, but six months from now, you will thank me."

"If you say so," Emily said, not buying it.

"You are going to meet some of the most accomplished, remarkable people in the world," Don said. "This is the opportunity of a lifetime! The contacts that you make from this will serve you forever. More important, you are going to learn from some of the world's most generous people how and why well-defined values around generosity have been so critical for their success. Not just professional success. I mean success as human beings. I envy you. I wish I could do it. I love these people."

"Then why *don't* you do it, if it's so enviable?" Emily asked, trying to keep the sarcasm out of her voice.

He laughed out loud. "It would be fun. And it's an all-star list of people to go see. But I've had my time with them. It's time for someone new to pick up where I've left off and take the knowledge and wisdom to a new level."

"Couldn't this all be done on Zoom?" Emily asked.

Don shook his head. "You want to be in the room with these folks," he explained. "Breathe the same air. That's how Napoleon Hill did it when he wrote *Think and Grow Rich*. That's how Ed Mylett interviews a vast majority of his podcast guests. Anyway, I think this will be a great growth experience for you. Didn't you write something in your VMVP about always wanting to grow?"

"You got me there," Emily said quietly. "It really sounded like some sort of way to get me to quit."

"That is as far from the truth as can be," Don said, holding out his arms to emphasize the point.

At that moment, the server brought the lattes and the croissants.

"It may seem crazy now," Don said, "but I promise you, after you have done the first couple of interviews, you will be saying to yourself, 'Don was right. This really is the opportunity of a lifetime.'"

Emily pondered his words, nodded thanks to the server, glanced at the waves lapping at the sand and the runners on the beach, and sipped her drink.

"I'm going to miss these lattes," she said, "not to mention the view."

Don thanked the server and turned his attention back to Emily.

"Any questions?" he asked. She shook her head.

"I will get you a list of interviewees and we'll establish dates. You will make your own travel arrangements and bill the company, or we'll make them for you. You are going to be a busy person, but you will also have time to reflect and think about the future."

"The company is really going to create a position called Chief Generosity Officer?" Emily asked, studying Don. "Is that for real?"

"As real as I'm sitting here," Don assured her. "It was actually my team's idea, but I loved it. We believe that generosity is the most underrated key to success in life, in business, in family, personal achievement, happiness. And, in this changing world we live in, particularly as technology advances, person-to-person generosity will become even more important because it's what will make our human touch and attention to relationships stand out. We basically want somebody to evangelize values and the power of generosity throughout the enterprise. And as coincidence would have it, there I was looking at your performance, hearing reports about what was really going on, and trying to figure out what to do with you, young lady."

> "In this changing world we live in, person-to-person generosity will become even more important."

Despite her misgivings about the whole mission, Emily had to laugh.

"Young lady?" she asked. "What am I, your daughter all of a sudden?"

"This isn't how we typically speak in the corporate world," Don said, "but the setting, with the beach and the bay...this isn't the most corporate of locations. So yes, I do feel somewhat like a father figure to you. You were still pretty wet behind the ears when we first met."

"Is there anything else?" she asked, sighing. "Because I *know* you. With you, there is *always* one more thing."

Don looked as though he suddenly remembered something.

"Read this," he said, taking a folded piece of paper out of his jacket pocket and handing it to Emily. "Read it out loud to me."

Emily, intrigued, unfolded the paper and started to read.

"*Passion.* My passion is to travel and see the world and embrace the role of being a productive global citizen."

Emily paused and looked up. "That sounds very idealistic now, but I recognize this," she said. "Why exactly am I reading this?"

Don smiled. "Keep reading," he said, his tone encouraging.

"*Vision:* to be known as a leader and a visionary person in my field," Emily continued. "To be fully valued. To be both financially successful and recognized by my peers and the people I work with. Down the road to be a great spouse and mom, and a pillar of my community. To support others in my world in their spiritual, professional, or psychological growth."

She looked at him, confused, as if to say, Why are we doing this?

"Keep going," Don said, leaning back comfortably and sipping his latte.

"*Mission,*" Emily continued. "Mission. To serve. To help my fellow men and women when they are away from home, either because they are traveling for work and must be at their best, or because they are on vacation and want to create memories to last a lifetime. I will pursue opportunities through the company as well as sports. I will share my story and the lessons I have learned through speaking and writing, while continuing to learn from the stories and experiences of others. I will be financially independent by age forty. I will show the people I work with how they can achieve financial independence as well."

Emily hesitated and blinked a couple of times.

Don sat impassively, waiting for her to continue. She kept reading.

Values. Core beliefs.

I believe:

- In complete honesty.
- In investing in the success of others.
- In hard work and being a loyal teammate when at play or work.
- In being kind always.
- In doing my best always and producing great results.
- That success depends on being in control of my emotions and never letting fear or anxiety run me.
- In committing to personal growth in every way.
- I will achieve career success and financial freedom.

Don waited. And then the penny dropped.

"_I guess this says it all!_" Emily admitted, staring at him. "This is _my_ VMVP. My Vision, Mission, Values, and Passion. You made me do this when I was still an intern, before I graduated Cornell. It was very aspirational, but most of this still holds true."

Don smiled. "I have wondered whatever became of that young woman," he said teasingly. "Have you seen her?"

Emily gave Don a reproving look, as if to say, Cut that out.

"Okay, oh wise one," Emily said, smiling for the first time in days. "I see you working. This is what you had me draw up back in the day. You're giving it to me now to remind me that maybe I have gotten away from it. Which explains why I'm getting fired from this beautiful property even though I brought the profit up."

Don just grinned. She got it.

"And it's all about *how* I got the profit up," Emily said, looking serious again. "You are saying I got away from what is most important and who I am. And you are saying that if I start talking to all these smart people about their wisdom around generosity, I will learn a lot. But I will also find myself again. Is that what I'm hearing?"

Don drained his latte and ignored his croissant.

"You nailed it," he said, smiling. "You will be searching for guidance about the many dimensions of generosity, and then if it all works out, you are going to take what you learn and teach it company-wide. But just as important, and perhaps more important, you are going to be searching for Emily.

"You are going to reconnect with the generous, idealistic young lacrosse star I met at an open house at Cornell so many years ago. That is why I'm sending you, and not someone else, on this very special mission."

"Well, when you put it like that..." Emily said, and she could feel her shoulders lowering for the first time in days. The tension was draining out of her body. She sighed, and she suddenly felt herself in tune with Don, with the company, with the waves hitting the beach, with the universe. Don had a way of making you feel good about yourself and about what he wanted for you.

"When is my first interview?" Emily asked. "Who all am I talking to?"

Don reached back into his jacket pocket and pulled out an envelope. He slid it across the table to Emily.

"You will find all the names and some proposed dates in here," he said. "I've chatted with each and they are expecting to hear from you. I'm glad you are feeling better about things. This wasn't fun for either of us, up until now. But I think you are about to go on the greatest adventure of your life so far."

Emily picked up the envelope, tapped it on the table, and grinned.

"I like the sound of that!" she exclaimed. "Here's to new beginnings!"

Don smiled and raised his empty cup.

"To new beginnings!" he repeated. "Okay, you've got your work cut out for you. I've got to get back to the office for a call."

He gave her a friendly nod, wrapped his croissant in a napkin, tossed a five-dollar bill onto the table as a tip, stood, smiled again, and departed.

Emily glanced at the envelope, which contained her future, or at least her plans for the next six months.

She looked up again.

Don was already gone.

CHAPTER 4

YOU BET YOUR BIPPY

Emily awakened the next morning at 5:30 a.m. without the benefit of an alarm clock, as she had practically every morning since moving to San Diego. She lay there in the darkness, doing what she did first thing every morning—recalling the list of tasks she needed to accomplish, crises that needed resolution, long-range plans she wanted to discuss with her management team, and so on. For some strange reason today, however, nothing came to mind.

She sighed, feeling frustrated, and turned over, hoping to go back to sleep since she didn't have to be up at the crack of dawn. Or up at all, for that matter. She could sleep until noon and no one would care. The thought did not bring her joy. Emily loved working, and she loved her property. It felt as though something precious had been ripped away from her. She didn't want to sleep, she didn't want to get up, and most of all, she didn't want to cry.

After a few more fitful snatches at additional sleep, she resigned herself to the fact that she would have to get up and face a day with no work in it. She didn't think of herself as a workaholic. She just thought of herself as someone deeply dedicated to her role. And now she didn't have a role, unless you counted this whole crazy generosity business from Don. A part of her still believed that it was a make-work project, the purpose of which was to induce her to quit so the company wouldn't have to fire her.

Don had told her repeatedly that the project was real, and she desperately wanted to believe him. It just seemed so far from anything she had ever heard of in the corporate world. Chief Generosity Officer? Who are we kidding here? She sighed, got out of bed, and flipped on the light.

She put some coffee on and checked her texts, even though she assumed there would be nothing, itself a strange departure from her normal routine. She typically woke up with ten to twenty texts from team members or from corporate, and at least as many emails. It always seemed daunting to cope with all that incoming, but Emily actually loved it. She loved being engaged, she loved working with people, and she loved making her property better and more successful. She had never told anyone, but she thought of Pinafore San Diego as her own personal bonsai tree, which she pruned, and grew, and cared for not just with hard work or massive action but with what she thought at the time was love. This made it all the harder to see that she had only one message on her phone.

Of course, it was from Don:

You've got your first meeting one week from today. Details to follow. You'll be doing them all in person. For something this important, in person is essential. Get your research going.

Emily read and reread the text and shook her head. *Seriously?* In person? Since the pandemic, practically everything was done via Zoom or Teams.

It was such a relief when business travelers, and then vacationers, started to hit the road again. Those were some lean years at her property and for the hospitality industry in general. What was so important about generosity that it couldn't be handled on a video call, like pretty much everything else these days? Emily shook her head, still not buying the whole thing.

Emily had enjoyed morning yoga on the beach and often attended a class that the property offered to its guests. That way, she could get in an hour of yoga and also talk to some guests about how their visit was going. Two birds with one stone. This morning, she dressed for yoga but headed to a part of the beach far from the resort. She did not want to run into any teammates. Too awkward.

When Emily had first moved to San Diego, the company had put her up in one of those executive suite places, a furnished unit that offered all of the requirements of the business traveler and few of the comforts of home. Emily had always been so busy that she never found time to look for her own place. Her former boyfriend who had visited a few times had mentioned that it felt so transient. Emily agreed and regularly promised herself that she would find somewhere homier. Somehow, she never got around to it. Now, she wasn't even sure if she would stay in San Diego. Who knew what her future held? She tried to put all those thoughts out of her mind and typed the word *generosity* into Google.

The first thing that came up was the dictionary definition, "The quality of being kind and generous." From somewhere in her educational career, most likely middle school, Emily remembered a rule against using the same word in its own definition. She took this as a bad sign. If generosity was defined as "The quality of being kind and generous," if generosity meant being generous, in other words, how much could there really be to say about it? She scrolled up and found that there were about 183,000,000 results. She sighed. Maybe there was more to say about generosity. Whatever. She dug in.

Next stop: Wikipedia, of course. Why not? Usually you just found restatements of the blindingly obvious, but sometimes Wikipedia could serve up a nugget. "Generosity is regarded as a virtue by various world religions and philosophies, and is often celebrated in cultural and religious ceremonies," she read.

Duh, she thought. Then there was a reference to oxytocin, the internal chemical that the body fired off when it was happy. That's interesting. Then some material about the etymology of the word, which did not interest her. Generosity in religion. In philosophy. She sighed again. The whole thing felt like going down a rabbit hole. Was Don really serious?

She reached for her phone and texted him: Is this for real?

Those infamous three dots indicating she was about to receive a return text, or possibly not, appeared, followed by the words: You bet. Keep the faith. Take this seriously. I do.

Emily decided to focus her search efforts by combining the word *generosity* with the phrase "hospitality industry." Among the many hits was a podcast with Danny Meyer. She knew that name. He was a legend in the industry. He helped launch Shake Shack. What would he have to say? She clicked and found that it was fifty-six minutes long and titled "The Intersection between Hospitality and Humanity." Well, if Danny Meyer had something to say about generosity, she wanted to hear it.

Efficient at multitasking, Emily kept on searching for other interesting links while listening to the podcast. What was this? A medical journal study from the National Institutes of Health? On generosity? *My tax dollars at work*, she thought scornfully. She clicked on the link and read the article.

She paused the podcast because she found herself captivated by the idea that there could be psychological or health benefits from generosity.

Next, she searched "generosity and happiness." She found a course on the subject at Yale called The Pursuit of Happiness, which turned out to be the most popular class at Yale. Really?

Next up, a *Forbes* magazine interview with Adam Grant titled "Seven Ways That Generosity Can Lead to Success." Emily was not a fan of all those articles that talked about the five tools or the seven whatevers. On the other hand, Adam Grant was a thinker she respected. She read all his books, and then she remembered that one of them, *Give and Take*, was at its core all about the power of generosity.

Maybe there's more of this topic than I thought, she decided, reading the Adam Grant interview.

Next, she went back to it, putting it in a list of references and links so that she could return to them later if she so desired. She could also send it to Don, to show him that she was taking the whole project seriously, or at least as seriously as she could manage.

She next googled "emotions and generosity" and found a ton of links to articles that looked interesting. "Health Benefits of Giving to Others." "Why Generosity Is Good for You." "Generosity and the Helper's High." "Studies of Functional MRIs of Givers." Seriously? Who has time to do all this kind of research?

Then she found this statement: "Generous individuals are personally more fulfilled, happier and more peaceful within themselves, not to mention more productive at home and in the workplace." That came from an article on MidlandHealth.com, whatever that was.

> "Generous individuals are personally more fulfilled, happier and more peaceful within themselves."

The time began to fly as Emily found link after link, podcast after podcast, video after video, all offering different insights on the value of generosity. Generosity not only directly benefited others but also made you happier, healthier, and just a better person all around. She felt as if she had slipped into one of those old *Saturday Night Live* reruns with Stuart Smalley talking about what a good person you are (and doggone it, people *like* you!).

But this stuff was for real. Another study. The more she read, the more she realized that Don was right. There was a lot here. Much more than she had ever expected. What about in the business world? She fired up LinkedIn and searched for posts on generosity, and it didn't take long before she found business professionals describing how being generous had helped them in their careers. Generous people actually earn more money, according to one writer. Generous leaders produce better results. *If you say so*, Emily thought, not yet convinced. It just sounded like everybody wanted to say great things about generosity, just so that it would sound good. At the same time, however, she could not diminish the sincerity and credibility of the people who were writing about generosity in such stirring terms.

> **"Generous leaders produce better results."**

It began to sound as though generosity was some sort of superpower, she decided, which strengthened givers just as the givers improved the lives of the people to whom they gave. So many implications to all of this if it's true.

She texted Don: Is generosity a superpower?

Those three burbling dots came back, followed by a quick reply from Don: You bet your bippy.

Emily laughed out loud. *You bet your bippy? Are you kidding me?*

She checked the clock and saw that it was almost noon. She looked out the window. The marine layer had burned off. What if she went for a run and listened to the rest of the Danny Meyer podcast? She sighed. It wasn't as if she had anything better to do. And this stuff was kind of interesting, she had to admit.

She got her running shoes on, hopped back in her Jeep, and headed to a hilly trail a couple of miles from her home. That was the beautiful thing about San Diego—you were surrounded by nature in all its glory. Mountains, hills, desert, ocean, bay. Not to mention SeaWorld and Legoland if you had kids, which she didn't, but certainly many of the guests did. Even though she had never been to either, she had described them so often that she felt as though she knew them like the back of her hand. Not that that information would do her any good at this point.

Don't be bitter, she told herself. *They could have just fired you.*

She never worked out twice in one day, but today was not a normal day. Emily ran through the barren hills for almost an hour, listening to the podcast. The subject was far more interesting, and far more complex, than she had imagined. When she got home, she showered and changed, made a salad for lunch, then went back to her laptop. Instead of reading, she started to make some notes.

Generosity equals superpower?

1. Generosity creates karma.
2. Not about expectation of return.
3. A spirit of generosity is a way of life?
4. Even a smile is generosity. Humility is big generosity.
5. Helping others.
6. Teach a man to fish, don't just give them food. Altruism is different?
7. Builds trust and relationships—revisit that Harvard study.

8. Creates joy.
9. Nothing generous about blame. Stop blaming.
10. Self-generosity. Being generous to yourself.

Emily stopped typing and instead stared at the last words she had typed: self-generosity. She looked around her executive suite. It wasn't bad—there was nothing wrong with it—but it wasn't exactly a shining example of self-generosity.

Maybe there were a few things she could learn that might help her in her own life.

By now it was two o'clock and Emily had been working for seven hours—eight if you included the run while she was listening to the podcast. Her energy dipped in the late afternoon, which is when she would normally head out to the veranda overlooking the Pacific to grab a latte, recharge, and get ready to power through the rest of her day. But today she felt a twinge of regret that she couldn't score her usual table with that awe-inspiring view that somehow never got old.

She thought about making more coffee, but her mind went back to that phrase she had just typed. Self-generosity.

Emily suddenly realized that she had been through a lot in the last few days. A lot of emotion. A lot of change.

She decided to draw inspiration from the work that she had done and be generous to herself. Emily did something that she had never done on a workday since leaving college.

She went back to bed.

CHAPTER 5

ENDLESS REWARDS:
WILL LITTLE

Emily looked out of the airplane's window and saw the city of Denver spread out before her, surrounded by a C-shaped range of faraway mountains. It was definitely a city, with a skyline of new and aging office towers, but to Emily's surprise, it looked a lot like a smaller Los Angeles, with its San Fernando Valley to the east instead of the north.

The pilot announced the plane's imminent landing. One last time, Emily wiggled around in her first-class seat, luxuriating in the width and comfort before she pulled her seat belt more snugly. Even on this two-hour flight, she'd been handed a free drink and given some snacks—not prepackaged!—on a real plate. Emily hadn't realized she was flying first class until she'd arrived at San Diego International with her rolling bag and briefcase. The machine that issued her boarding pass knew, though, and there it was, FIRST CLASS, in big red letters. Don must have upgraded her flight at the last minute. Emily sailed through check-in and found her gate. Right next to it was the first-class lounge for her airline, and she ventured in, feeling almost like an impostor. *Pinafore didn't have to fly me first class*, Emily thought as she helped herself to some fruit. She'd always flown coach and expected to this time. *I guess that's generosity, huh? I could get used to this.*

At Denver International, Emily was walking toward ground transportation when she noticed a uniformed greeter holding up a card with her name on it. "Hello, Ms. Gardner," he said when she approached. "Is that all your luggage?"

"It is," Emily said. "I'm just staying overnight."

They headed for the exit.

"Is this your first trip to Denver?" the greeter asked.

"Yes," Emily said.

"Well, it's a beautiful city, lots to see," he said. "If you like beer, go out tonight and try one of our breweries. Denver is famous for them. But don't go until about seven; rush hour is murder around here."

"Thanks for the heads-up."

At the curb, a liveried driver had a town car waiting. *OMG*, Emily thought. *I was going to take an Uber. I guess this is generosity too.* "Well, Ms. Gardner, I'll leave you in this gentleman's hands," the greeter said, immediately melting into the crowd.

The driver opened the back door for Emily, then put her rolling bag in the trunk. "Welcome to Denver," he said as he pulled away from the curb.

"Thanks," Emily said. "Do we have time to stop at my hotel before we go to the Tech Center?"

Her meeting with Will Little was at noon.

"Yes, ma'am," the driver said. "The hotel is just outside the Tech Center and has you cleared for early check-in."

Emily nodded and watched the passing landscape avidly. A lot of empty space, mostly sunburnt, tawny grass as they left the airport. It took about forty minutes for the town car to pull up to the Pinafore hotel, one of the most imposing in a row of late-model, high-end hotels. After the driver set down Emily's rolling bag, she asked him to give her ten minutes as she walked into the hotel to check in.

"Ms. Gardner, of course! We've been looking forward to your visit," said the clerk behind the counter. Emily, trained to inspect and evaluate hotel employees, gazed approvingly at the crisp uniform and the big name tag the young woman wore. "Thank you, Violet," she said. She looked around the immaculate lobby, white and beige with dashes of color in some of the chairs and the wall art, noting its combination of majesty, productivity, and comfort. *Nice*, she thought.

The suite was nice too: perfectly clean, laminated list of TV stations under a plastic-wrapped remote, bed made beautifully with top-line linens. The sitting room had a comfortable but clean sofa and another TV, and abstract paintings rather than landscapes and cutesy cottage scenes added an air of sophistication. It gave Emily a little pang, though: *This is what my apartment looked like when I first moved in.* Since Emily didn't have to change clothes, she just made sure her hair was in place and was back to the car in the promised ten minutes.

The hotel was at the edge of the Denver Technological Center; Shea Properties, the company Will Little worked for, had bought the Tech Center in 2006. Shea was a division of the J. F. Shea Co., a monstrous, fifth-generation family-owned company that started out as a plumbing contractor in 1881 and grew to be the largest private homebuilder in the US. The construction division had worked on many of America's most challenging engineering projects, including the Hoover Dam, the Golden Gate and Oakland Bay bridges in San Francisco, the Bay Area Rapid Transit system, and new parts of the Metro system in Los Angeles.

Shea Properties owned and operated some ten thousand apartment units and millions of square feet of commercial real estate space.

Denver Tech Center went on for miles, shiny office towers interspersed with low-slung buildings and acres of green space, much of its grounds covered with trees. Emily noticed that many of the buildings had patios with tables, chairs, and benches outside, pleasant places for employees to eat lunch and get a breath of air. She expected Shea's headquarters to occupy a few floors in one of the glass-clad towers and was almost disappointed when the town car stopped at the entrance of a two-story gray building that looked a bit like a converted warehouse or gym.

After thanking the driver, Emily went to the front desk and told the receptionist she had an appointment with Will Little. "Yes, he's expecting you," the receptionist said after checking her screen. "Go right up. His office is at the top of the stairs to the right, or there's an elevator behind me."

Though the outside of the building was modest, the inside was new and beautiful. It was clearly designed to do business. Up the stairs—and catching her breath in the mile-high altitude—she found Little's office immediately. Its door was ajar, but Emily knocked anyway and went in when invited. Will Little, seated at his desk, rose immediately in greeting.

"I'm Emily from Pinafore Hotels, Mr. Little," she said.

"Please call me Will," he replied. "May I call you Emily?"

"Of course, Will. Thanks for taking the time to meet with me."

Little was younger than Emily had pictured, probably early forties. She had seen his photo on Shea's website, of course, but had figured it to be an old picture. Corporate executives were often older than their online photos, something Emily had realized early in her career. She'd made a point of looking up prominent businesspeople before they checked into the hotels she'd worked at so she'd know something about them, and as a result had seen a few execs come through who were fortyish and great-looking online but ten to thirty years older in real life. Little had some gray at the temples and in his short beard, but he looked younger than Don.

He was a pretty impressive guy for any age, actually. Little started out working as a manager for a general contractor but decided he wanted to be in real estate development, so logically he became a general contractor for real estate developers. When the recession of 2008 hit, Little moved over to a strategic consulting company, and after a few years there, an old contracting client asked him to manage the design and construction process for a Denver-based development company responsible for some of Colorado's great mountain resorts. It was a plum job, but eventually Little moved to Shea so he could travel less and be exposed to a wider variety of projects. As Shea's senior vice president of acquisitions and development, he was clearly on a fast track.

"Why don't we sit at the table?" Little said. "I think we'll both be more comfortable there than at my desk."

Little's office was large but somewhat modest, which seemed to be consistent with Don's description of Little's personality. They settled themselves at a nice table in the corner. "I kind of thought you'd be in one of the office towers," Emily said.

"No, we chose this building because it was centrally located in the Tech Center, and directly adjacent to our newest project," Little said. "It used to be a 24-Hour Fitness, and we remodeled it to accommodate more than fifty employees. I like that we kept a gym and locker room on the premises," he added. "I work out here every morning."

And it shows, Emily thought, admiring Little's wiry build. "So you know that Pinafore is sending me around the United States to interview executives and companies known for their generosity," she said.

"Well, you came to the right place," Little said. "I am fortunate to be surrounded by extremely generous people in every aspect of my life.

I'm not exactly sure why I was given this blessing, but it's enhanced my life in every way. My family, my wife, my friends, and the companies I have worked for, especially Shea, inform my entire outlook.

"Shea has been incredibly successful, but the people I know in the company, including its owners, are extremely humble, some of the most bighearted people you could ever meet. They're unassuming, down-to-earth, very genuine—amazing people. They are also very generous."

"And that generosity reaches beyond giving money to causes?" Emily asked.

"That's right," Little said. "It's bigger than philanthropy. Giving money is sometimes the easiest thing to do, right? It requires very little emotional or intellectual commitment. Writing a check is relatively painless, and the government rewards you for doing it most of the time. Everybody thinks that's what generosity is, but I would argue that is probably the easiest and least impactful. You get the email asking you to donate, and you do, and you don't think another thing about it.

"I think true generosity comes from giving something that costs you more than money; typically, you're giving your time or emotional energy. Generosity means putting in the effort to have an impact on something larger than yourself. And you gain from generosity. People to whom you're generous eventually give you their trust, and when people begin to trust you, they give you opportunity and greater influence in their lives and in the lives of others. I'm not generous for that reason, but I know it to be how it works."

> "Generosity means putting in the effort to have an impact on something larger than yourself."

Emily nodded, thinking about how much time it took to send that heavy coat from Hong Kong to Ulan Bator.

"Some of the most rewarding experiences I've had in my personal life and career have been opportunities to help other people," Little said. "I've been shown how to mentor and have personally witnessed the benefit of someone mentoring me. I have been very fortunate, largely due to the generosity of others. There are many people that are just as smart, and just as hardworking, but what separates us in success is the generosity of the people in my life who have helped pave the path to success."

"Very fortunate. Can you give me an example of an opportunity you were given?" Emily asked.

"Well, the job I have now," Little said. "The Shea Senior Team had been in place for twenty years with virtually no change, which is pretty amazing. They hired me to help enable the next generation of success. They hired me for my experience, of course, but more so for who I am and my fit within an organization that thrives on being humble and thoughtful. They brought me on to be a leader. The trust they showed me is something I will never forget and always work to protect."

"That says a lot for them," Emily said.

"It sure does," Little replied. "They made a conscious decision to bring in a different way of thinking and a fresh approach to culture, because the world's changing, and our business is changing, and in order to do that, we need to blend our existing strategies with some new thoughts and new ideas. They weren't thinking about themselves. They were thinking about everybody else who wants a lifelong career here and how they can ensure that those people are going to be successful."

"That must make Shea unusual," Emily suggested.

"Actually, I don't think so, just from my own work experience," Little said. "Every opportunity I've had to grow in my career has been a function of someone who has trusted me and who was looking out for a much larger group of people than just themselves. They were trying to grow a business and provide opportunities for people whom they knew and loved. Could they have had economic benefit from that? Absolutely. But there are easier ways to make money than continuing to add people and grow payroll. We have to keep those people employed. We have to make sure that they are fulfilled, that they have jobs that they love. To do this, you really need to genuinely care and want to help people. It's a big responsibility."

"I'm told the way you allocate space to employees is part of Shea's generous practices," Emily said.

"I would say so," Little said modestly. "At least in this building, we don't believe in corner offices. I'm sure you've noticed that this office has no windows. No one on the senior team has a window to the outside. Those offices go to younger team members so they can have daylight and a view outside, things that enhance the work environment."

Emily smiled. "Maybe *you're* the outlier, Will."

She was teasing, but Little took her seriously.

"It's possible. I come from a long line of very generous people. And I'm very lucky. All four of my grandparents lived till I was thirty-four. My mother's parents lived to their midnineties. My father's father passed away recently, but not only was he ninety-two, he still went to the office almost every day of the work week. Dad's mother is still with us, and still raising hell, which is awesome."

Emily looked at him wide-eyed. She had only one grandparent left, too, but her grandmother had dementia and didn't even know her anymore. In addition, Emily was at least fifteen years younger than Little.

"My father's father was a very successful businessman," he was saying, "and made it a point to donate a significant amount of his money to help other people. He was always involved in community efforts that he thought were important. He grew up very poor and worked incredibly hard to get where he was, but if he were sitting here, he would tell you that his success had a lot more to do with generosity than it did with hard work. He would say this to me often, knowing it would help me in life.

"My grandfather went into a business whose owner was amazingly helpful to him, who provided him with incredible opportunities and even made him a partner. Because my grandfather was the beneficiary of extreme generosity, he felt it was important to pass that on to people who were outside of our family.

"My parents are like that too," Little continued. "They're both in health care. They gave me and my siblings every material thing we needed and put us all through school, but they also taught us the work ethic we needed to be successful and exemplified giving their time and resources to help people in impoverished countries get access to health care.

"My father still volunteers at a free clinic a couple of days a week and provides free medical services for people in his community. My mom's father volunteered most days of the week after he retired from the insurance business, but before that, he and my grandmother made a point to help take care of not only the people in their employ but often the families of those people as well."

"Wow," Emily said. "So you've known generosity in your personal life as well as in your work life."

"Wait, I'm not done," Little said. "I haven't told you about my wife. I had been married before and was sure I didn't want to do that again, but then I met Sara up in Aspen. Not only was she beautiful, but she's the most giving person I've met in my entire life. She would give the shoes off her feet, the shirt off her back, to anyone who needed them.

"Sara was a single mother of four when I met her, and the fact that she could clothe and feed children in a town like Aspen was a miracle to start with. Couple that with the fact that she was actively involved in charity and giving her time to the church and other organizations. It blew me away. I was struck by how enriched her life was by her generosity and how she wasn't looking to get anything back. It was amazing to me how happy she was in what were less-than-ideal circumstances, because she chose to give of every resource she had."

"She sounds wonderful," Emily said. *Good God, she raised four kids in Aspen. Until recently, I couldn't afford to walk down the street in Aspen.*

"She is, and her kids are great, too," Little said. "I was diagnosed very young with a degenerative neuromuscular disease that, miraculously, I grew out of, although it gave me a lot of trouble when I was a boy. I figured I would never have kids, because I didn't want to take a chance of passing on the disease, especially if the child *didn't* grow out of it.

"Sara's children became my children, and I can tell you that being a part of their lives has been the most gratifying experience of my life. The reward is endless. And watching these children become young adults of character and morality has been amazing! Now that they are growing up, their social circles are connecting me with people whose interests and experiences overlap mine, and that's providing opportunities for me to have even greater impact. Things really do come full circle."

"That's something, to take on four kids like that," Emily said.

"I guess," Little admitted. "It was definitely time-consuming and expensive to suddenly be the father of four. But being around young people at home made me better equipped to talk to the younger people in our office, and there are a lot of them. The same training and thought processes and intention that have gone into raising kids also go into growing the careers of these young people. And frankly, that's the most rewarding part of my job. We are all happy to see a financially successful project, but what makes me even happier is seeing people who are new in their careers get truly excited about what we do."

This guy is a saint, Emily thought. *I can see why Don put him first on the list.*

"How are you generous to yourself?" she asked. "There must be things you have to do for yourself to give you the ability to be generous to others."

"That's a great question," Little said. "When I see people get burned out or lose their temper, when they don't have the bandwidth for the job that day, I know they aren't being generous with, or taking care of, themselves."

"So what do you do?"

"Mostly, I just keep myself healthy," Little said. "I eat healthy, get enough sleep, work out. I'm very protective of my workout time and the few minutes a day I need to be alone, quiet, and thoughtful. Then, too, our mutual friend Don helped me with defining my vision, mission, and values. As you probably know, he loves this stuff. Frankly, so do I. In order to be the best version of myself I first need to know who I am and ultimately who I want to be. Understanding these things is incredibly empowering."

Emily smiled. The pieces were starting to fall into place. "What else can you tell me about generosity?" she asked.

"Well, for me, anyway, I consider it an obligation, not an option," Little said. "I was raised in a religious household, and I was taught that the Lord's sacrifice of His life was the ultimate expression of generosity. I still believe that. I also think that you can't be generous with the expectation of receiving some benefit from it. You have to be generous for its own sake or because it's the right way to be.

"It may be years before you see any effect or benefit from your actions, if ever. That doesn't mean thoughtfulness isn't worth practicing. One more thing: to reiterate, generosity isn't about money.

Remember, it's mostly about time and kindness. A smile at the right time or a caring conversation are signs of generosity too. They can have a significant impact on someone's life."

"One more question," Emily said, unintentionally slipping into *Columbo* mode. "Do you think there's any science behind generosity and what makes it so powerful?"

"I don't know that I would call it science," Little said. "But I think there is certainly a cause-and-effect relationship. Generosity builds trust, and trust can yield a number of benefits. People will trust you to pay back money you borrow, for example, or be willing to hire you because they trust that you'll do the job well. It's not science, but I would say there is a very logical and rational approach and subsequent set of effects that come with it. I see that in our younger staff and in my kids. When I am generous, they are respectful, thoughtful, and generous in return."

> "Generosity builds trust, and trust
> can yield a number of benefits."

Emily wrapped up the meeting and thanked Little warmly. She walked through the Shea building with misgivings, though. *Is this what Don and Pinafore want from me? Am I supposed to become a saint?*

She looked at the employees on the first floor, trying to suss out whether they seemed happier than other office workers she had seen. It was hard to tell. Still, Will Little's way of doing business certainly was working for him.

When she left the building, Emily was surprised to see the same car and driver waiting for her. "Can I take you back to the hotel?" the driver asked.

"No, thank you," Emily said. "I'd like to go to the Art Museum."

She'd spent some time on the plane looking for sightseeing options.

"Sure," the driver said.

A thought crossed Emily's mind that hadn't occurred to her that morning. "What's your name?" she asked the driver.

"I'm Julio," he said.

"Did Pinafore hire you to chauffeur me around all day?"

"I'm not at liberty to say, ma'am," Julio said. "But I am at your disposal."

"Okay, Julio," Emily said. "I'm going to have lunch, look at some paintings, and walk over to the Molly Brown House. Can you pick me up there around four o'clock? You can take me back to the hotel, and the rest of the evening is yours."

Back at the hotel, after setting the time for Julio to drive her to the airport the next day, Emily changed into shorts and a tee and began her report to Don. She dutifully wrote up everything Little had talked about and ended the report:

Will Little may be a saint, but he's also a heckuva good businessman.

CHAPTER 6

A SPORTING CHANCE:
LEIGH STEINBERG

Emily smiled as she sailed past the UC Irvine campus in her Jeep Cherokee, the car to which she'd treated herself when she took the position in San Diego. She was making great time—everyone who was going to the beach must have already arrived—and she wasn't making a white-knuckled ascent or descent at San Diego International. This interview was in Orange County, just up the road. Well, two hours up the road from her apartment. Google Maps said 1:34, but that would be at about 3:00 a.m. on a Sunday.

She drove to the end of Route 55 and turned onto the short stretch of Pacific Coast Highway between the freeway and the Leigh Steinberg Sports offices. After pulling into the parking lot under the building, she found a visitor's space, then the elevator to the third floor. *I'm looking forward to this*, Emily thought. She'd been a sports fan all her life but had never really met anyone important in the world of professional sports. Teams that came into San Diego tended to stay at Hiltons and Marriotts close to the stadiums and arenas, so a top athlete rarely checked into the Pinafore.

Just before she entered Steinberg's office, she checked her phone and found a lengthy text from Don:

Not to put any pressure on you, but Leigh is a pretty special guy. He used his propensity and desire to be generous to influence an entire industry. He was trailblazing in helping athletes enhance their lives and the lives of others through community engagement and athlete-sponsored charitable foundations. He and his team made generosity a selling advantage by recognizing that successful athletes want to give back and want to make a difference. They created a system that helped athletes redirect huge amounts of money and attention toward outstanding philanthropic purposes and become more successful in life at the same time. If it weren't for Leigh, this may never have happened, certainly not on such a universal scale.

No need to be nervous, but that's who you're dealing with!

Emily absorbed the text, swallowed hard, and entered Steinberg's suite.

The view even from the receptionist's desk was incredible: blue ocean as far as Emily could see, dotted with motorboats and the occasional yacht. The young man at the desk said Mr. Steinberg had just stepped out but invited Emily to wait. She dropped her briefcase on a chair and went to the window overlooking the ocean in the distance and the bay below. The view was even more spectacular from Steinberg's wall-to-wall, floor-to-ceiling window: the same ocean view, but uninterrupted, and below, in the bay, hundreds of boats, every size, shape, and color, and hundreds of people eager to get out on the water.

When Emily turned around, she saw that Steinberg's office was a sports fan's wonderland. Every surface and shelf was covered with memorabilia from a fifty-year career and back even further: The 1955 Brooklyn Dodgers were represented by a crowd of little ceramic figures. There were autographed footballs, baseballs, helmets, and boxing gloves. The walls were covered with photos of Steinberg with famous athletes, film stars, and beyond. Steinberg with Matt Damon. Steinberg with Cuba Gooding Jr. and Tom Cruise—Steinberg was widely assumed to have been the model for Cruise's title character in the 1996 movie *Jerry Maguire* and had a cameo in the film. Steinberg inducting Warren Moon into the Pro Football Hall of Fame. Steinberg and Barack Obama. Photo after photo of instantly recognizable celebrities, plus dozens of awards. One shelf even displayed products featuring athletes on their labels: Ben Roethlisberger's barbecue sauce, Patrick Mahomes's breakfast cereal.

Emily was looking at the box of Mahomes Magic Crunch when Steinberg entered the office. He was wearing a polo shirt and khakis, looking twenty years younger than his actual age. *Whoa*, Emily thought. *That's how I want to look when I'm in my seventies.*

"You must be Ms. Gardner," Steinberg said, extending his hand.

"I am, Mr. Steinberg," Emily said.

"Please, I'm Leigh," he said.

"Okay, Leigh. I'm just Emily," she replied, smiling. "Quite a place you have here."

"Bunch of dust-catchers," Steinberg said modestly. "They'd make a helluva yard sale, though."

He invited Emily to sit with him at a small table under a large map of the United States.

"Tell me about this endeavor of yours," Steinberg said, leaning forward, indicating his interest in what promised to be an unusual conversation for him.

"Pinafore has asked me to speak with leaders who have a strong sense and history of generosity," Emily said. "You made the list because you have a well-documented track record of working with athletes who came into the professional sports world with a measure of idealism and morality and teaching them to give back to their communities."

"Yeah, that's pretty much been my passion," Steinberg said casually.

"Well, you know my boss, Don," Emily continued. "He wants to find a way to reach people, especially younger people, who are a big segment of our employee roster. We know that adults under age forty have a tremendous desire to be generous but often don't know how or even exactly why."

"Okay," Steinberg said, nodding. "And why did they send you particularly on this assignment?"

Emily was nonplussed for a moment. *What can I say that doesn't make me look bad?* she thought. *Oh, what the hell.*

"Don didn't think I had exhibited enough generosity of spirit," she admitted quickly. "I think he figured I'm young enough to be swayed by people who have lived the concept and I have the right combination of traits and ambition to truly try to understand."

"Oh, they want *you* to be more generous," Steinberg said with a chuckle. "How's that going? Is anything rubbing off?"

"Absolutely," Emily admitted. "It's early, but the more people I talk to, the more I learn. And I guess the more I realize I still need to learn too."

"So, what would you like to know?" Steinberg said, relaxing in his chair.

"Let's start with your upbringing," Emily said. "Did you come from generous people?"

"That's an understatement," Steinberg replied. "My father had two core values. One was to treasure relationships, especially family, and the second was to try to make a meaningful difference in the world and help people who can't help themselves because you feel their pain.

"My dad knew that a lot of people weren't going to do the second one. He used to say to me, 'When you are looking for someone to make a change or right a wrong, and you keep waiting for some amorphous "they"—older people, political figures, people in authority—to change things or make them right, you could wait forever, son. *The "they" is you; you are the "they."*'

"That imbued me and my brothers with the idea that we were our brothers' and sisters' keepers, that they were our responsibility. We learned from my dad that if we saw suffering and injustice in the world, we needed to feel it and act to relieve it."

> "We learned from my dad that if we saw suffering and injustice in the world, we needed to feel it and act to relieve it."

"Very powerful," Emily murmured.

"Basically, he wanted us to have empathy," Steinberg said. "Not just seeing things from someone else's perspective but understanding their heart and mind. It could be something as simple as sitting with someone who's alone. It could be helping someone stand up to a bully, lending someone money, seeing someone through a crisis. It always meant being a good listener. And if you could go beyond that, to help solve a problem or inspire someone, all the better."

"So your father really raised you to think about other people," Emily said.

"Yeah," Steinberg said. "He was the same about money. He said it was a tool to do good with, that no matter how hard I worked, it wasn't *my* money. He said the value of money was to make life easier for people around you. My father taught us that if all you had was a plate of beans, but the person next to you was starving, you gave them your beans, because you'd find the next plate of beans somewhere, somehow."

"I'm surprised you and your brothers aren't all monks."

Steinberg laughed. "Three Jewish monks—that would be funny. My two brothers definitely fit the bill. Jim writes books and is a spiritual scholar, and Don had a forty-year career in public service, both in government and in NGOs. I understood the assignment too, though.

"From the very beginning of my work with athletes, I've chosen clients who are willing to give back to the community, to set up scholarship funds or work with their churches and Boys and Girls Clubs. Today we have academies and career conferences, with the purpose of training the next generation in ethics and values as well as the skills for successful careers."

"You mentored athletes in this way even in your twenties?" Emily asked.

"Yeah," Steinberg said. "It started when I signed my very first client, Steve Bartkowski. I knew Steve when he was a star quarterback for UC Berkeley and I was his dorm counselor while I attended law school. When Steve graduated in 1975, I had finished law school and became Steve's attorney. Steve was the number one draft pick that year and was going to play for the Atlanta Falcons.

"We flew into Atlanta, and the airport was lit up like a movie premiere, this huge crowd pushing against the police line, media everywhere. I realized that to millions of people across the country, athletes are venerated celebrities, larger than life. And I thought, if I could make it a practice to take those young men and women who would go back to their communities and do some good for people, and influence them to do that, together we would be a role model for giving back. I started looking not just for great players but for intelligent folks who showed real leadership and/or a desire to contribute to their communities."

Emily nodded. All she'd been thinking about since graduating Cornell was making money and climbing the corporate ladder.

"So Troy Aikman endowed a full scholarship at UCLA," Steinberg continued. "Warrick Dunn established Home for the Holidays, a program that makes the down payment on houses for single parents, when he was a rookie with Tampa Bay. I helped heavyweight champ Lennox Lewis to cut a public-service announcement called 'Real Men Don't Hit Women.'

"If Lennox Lewis says real men don't hit women, he might reach some rebellious adolescent who won't listen to parents or police or any other authority figure, but he will listen to a macho guy. If an athlete walks into a high school where there is a bullying problem, goes into the cafeteria and visits the table with the less popular kids or a student with a disability, he can help change the culture of that school. It makes a difference in the athletes' lives, too. They're developing their non-sports skills, which can be of use to them after retirement—the ones who don't go into sportscasting, anyway."

Emily smiled.

"In 1977," Steinberg recalled, "I teamed up with Rolf Benirschke, a placekicker for the San Diego Chargers, and we created Kicks for Critters, a program that benefited the department of Conservation and Research for Endangered Species, CRES, at the San Diego Zoo. We donated money every time Rolf kicked a field goal, and he challenged the community to match the fundraising. People would sign a pledge card and donate a certain amount per field goal, and the card would be posted on the wall of a local store.

"A successful businessman might pledge a thousand dollars per field goal, and a little kid might pledge a nickel. The local newspaper ran a 'Rolf-o-Meter' to keep track of the donations. We united an entire community behind this concept, and the money raised actually did help the zoo save endangered species.

"We weren't promoting football or saying how great it is to be an athlete. We were being role models for what an interactive citizen is supposed to do in society. Rolf had been a zoology major, working summers at the zoo, and his father, an animal pathologist, founded CRES. Rolf was a dedicated endangered-animal activist and stayed with Kicks for Critters for years after he retired and the charity morphed into Celebration for the Critters.

"Back when I started with Rolf, most players didn't have charities," Steinberg added. "Now, every athlete has at least a cause or even a charitable foundation. I'd like to think I helped get that started."

"Don't a lot of people just see this kind of activity as a gimmick?" Emily asked, thinking about the PR benefit to the athletes. "It gets them great publicity, but does it accomplish anything?"

"Sure it does," Steinberg replied, surprised by the question. "Every year, you have the direct impact of an athlete going to UCLA on scholarship when he otherwise wouldn't be able to, and you have single moms who would never be able to afford a home moving into houses with their kids. A lot of those people are going to pay forward that help, like, 'This athlete helped me, and someday, I'm gonna help someone else.' Same thing with young people who come to work as sports agents and attorneys.

"We get hundreds of calls from young people trying to break into our business. We can't answer them all, but quite a few we do, and why? Because by mentoring young people early in their careers, lending them a helping hand, they may remember that someone helped them and they will help the next person. You set up a system in which each person has individual responsibility to make our world a nicer world."

"But what about the general public?" Emily asked. "Do individuals who aren't helped directly respond?"

"Most don't, but some do," Steinberg said. "If a hundred thousand people saw that they could pledge a certain amount of money for every time Rolf Benirschke kicked a field goal, and just five people pledge a thousand dollars, and Rolf kicks five field goals during the season, that's twenty-five thousand bucks for research and conservation just from five wealthy people.

"If a thousand people, one in every hundred, pledged five dollars per field goal, that's another twenty-five thousand dollars. Fifty thousand dollars was a nice piece of change forty years ago, and theoretically, we could raise it from just a hundred and five people out of a hundred thousand. Kicks for Critters raised millions over the years."

"And this comes from your upbringing?"

"A lot of it does," Steinberg said, nodding. "This isn't noblesse oblige. I didn't grow up in a wealthy family. My father taught school and later became a school principal. Dad's biggest claim to fame is being on the Los Angeles Human Rights Commission. But he taught me to take responsibility and do what's right, no matter the consequences, and also to be aware of the people around me.

"Let me tell you a story. I went to elementary school across the street from a federal housing project. One day I heard these horrific squeals of pain coming from somewhere, and when I looked across the street, I saw a group of guys over on the front stoop of one of the houses torturing a dog. They were burning the dog with matches and doing all these awful things, kicking it, I don't know what else.

"I could feel the dog's pain and didn't understand why no one was helping it. At that moment, I knew it was my responsibility to save the dog's life, maybe. I ran over and put myself in the middle of these kids and told them to stop. They let the dog alone and started beating the heck out of me, but I got the dog and ran off with it, and the dog stopped crying. I think I was crying, but the dog stopped."

"That was really brave," Emily said.

"So part of it is being raised to take responsibility, and another part is to open yourself to the pain in the world. And there's another part to generosity that I may or may not have learned from my dad: that you have to put all of your focus and intensity into the moment you're living. You're not looking at your smartphone or worrying about what tomorrow will bring or what happened yesterday. There will be a different reality later, but for right now, every bit of focus goes into this moment."

> **"There's another part to generosity: you have to put all of your focus and intensity into the moment you're living."**

"What does being in the moment have to do with generosity?" Emily asked.

"It's part of being a good listener and an empathetic person," Steinberg said. "The first part of generosity is an awareness of the feelings and needs of others. From there you can develop the skill set for building trust, creating an atmosphere that makes a person feel comfortable revealing their deepest fears and greatest dreams. That requires patience and the ability to be genuinely yourself.

"I admit, this often goes against the grain of being an athlete," Steinberg continued. "We're supposed to be strong, show how tough we are, but that role isn't necessarily helpful when you have to be the listener and the encourager. You have to listen to text and subtext, not just the words but the underlying feeling, and that means learning about someone's background, hearing the tone of voice, watching body language. And then it also means doing acts of kindness, asking, *How can I enhance your life?*"

Emily was silent for a moment. There was a lot more to Steinberg's work than representing athletes, she realized. That was the aftereffect, not the reason for what he did.

"Do you consider your true legacy to be these projects that you and the athletes have set up?"

"Sure," Steinberg said. "I'm under no illusion that fame, newspaper clippings, articles, putting your name on a building, or anything like that actually travels with you to the next lifetime. I establish programs where the need is. For example, I put together a program that trains professionals how to spot hate groups and help their communities promote ethnic diversity and aid the police in combating hate. We've trained ten thousand people in cities across the country. I was supporting research on concussions among football players almost thirty years ago, way before it got any publicity. I've been getting involved with climate change."

"How do you decide which causes to support?" Emily asked. "After all, there are infinite ways to get involved, and even you must have limits to your capacity."

"It's true, you have to prioritize," Steinberg said. "You have to decide who has the biggest need and how much time you have to work with. You need to make a list and deal with issues one by one. You don't think *Oh, gosh, I have to save the world* and get overwhelmed. Just focus on one thing at a time. Ultimately, interaction by interaction, you will be able to make an impact.

"Remember, too, that I'm not doing all this work by myself," he continued. "I ask the people I represent to find a way to give back, so they're still promoting causes and setting up programs in their communities. I've always represented 'elite athletes of elite character,' and I really believe in that."

Emily carefully considered the complement of an elite professional with elite character. Clearly Leigh was a visionary.

"Okay, I have to ask this," Emily said. "You look incredible for a guy who's been in this business since 1975. What's your secret?"

"Thank you, and it isn't one secret," Steinberg replied. "I do put a lot of effort into being healthy and feeling good. It starts with understanding that your body is not a machine, so the nutrition you put into it has to be what makes you personally feel the best."

"No junk food?" Emily asked.

"A *little*," Steinberg admitted with a smile. "When you hang out with people much younger than you are, you're going to have a nacho or two. Being kind to yourself involves a treat every now and then."

"And what else?" Emily asked, intrigued.

"Exercise is key, of course. I have a Fitbit and try to take 15,000 steps every day, and I work with a physical trainer three times a week. You have to be physically active."

Emily thought about the gym-quality elliptical in her bedroom that she was using as a clothes rack.

"But mostly, you need to pay attention to your brain function," Steinberg was saying. "Everything in your body, every cell, is controlled by the brain, so you need to keep your brain in good shape. Sunlight has an impact on the brain, so you need to be exposed to sunlight every day. I take advantage of a lot of the new biomed treatments that have come along. I've done almost a hundred sessions of RTMS, repetitive transcranial magnetic stimulation, where you get a coil applied to your head that conducts an electric current into part of your brain. There is also biofeedback brain training, which stimulates neuroplasticity, the ability of your brain to adapt and change, even in older people."

"That sounds almost like what went on in Dr. Frankenstein's lab," Emily said, laughing.

"Closer to an MRI, and it works for me," Steinberg said, smiling in return. "I'm clearer and happier. I've also done two hundred sessions of hyperbaric oxygen, which is usually used for wound-healing and replacing oxygen lost to something like carbon monoxide poisoning.

But pure oxygen also stimulates the growth of new stem cells, collagen, and skin cells, so it can be beneficial in that way. I take a lot of supplements that are meant to improve cognitive ability, and I've gone for brain training at Lake Nona near Orlando, where they work on neuroplasticity.

"You also have to be able to laugh at yourself, maintain a sense of humor and of irony, and recognize how fragile life is. Years ago, I thought age seventy-three meant wearing Madras shorts, black socks, and black shoes, sitting on a park bench with drool coming out of my mouth, unable to do much of anything, and I swore I would never be like that. Now I *am* seventy-three, and I'm not like that, and very grateful that I have everything I thought would go away."

"Anything else you're grateful for?" Emily asked.

Steinberg looked around his office for a moment. "All of this," he said, gesturing. "I'd rather not be in an office, but when it's *this* office, and what this work has given me, I can't be anything but grateful. I'm surrounded by palm trees and water, and inside I have pretty plants and happy memories and fish tanks, all sorts of things that make me happy."

Wow, this guy is lucky, Emily thought—then remembered that he had seen his share of troubles too. "How about a parting statement before we wind up?" she asked.

"It all goes back to empathy and listening," Steinberg said. "The basic principles of sports agency have never changed. People think the whole key to representation is persuasion, being able to sell. But it's always been about listening. It's about creating an environment where a client feels comfortable enough to open up. We can peel back the layers of the onion and get beyond surface responses. Then I can understand your deepest hopes and dreams and your greatest anxieties and fears, and if we can make that emotional connection, it's an understanding that can last for a career and for life."

Emily thanked him and headed down to her car after the receptionist validated her parking. What Steinberg had said about listening
stayed with her, and she realized that she had really listened to him
and, although she had taken notes, she remembered everything he
talked about. Emily thought back to other conversations she'd had,
when five minutes later she couldn't remember the topic of discussion. She'd been only half-listening. *Wow*, she thought, *if I'd really been
listening to Don, I wouldn't have misinterpreted his reasons for sending me on
this assignment. I wouldn't have gone kicking and screaming.*

Once in her car, Emily peeled off her blazer and, in the shadows
of the deserted parking lot, her pantyhose. After leaving the building,
she was about to turn right, back to the freeway, but she looked out
at the water, now white with boats, and turned left onto poky old
Pacific Coast Highway. It would add at least a half hour to Emily's trip
home, but *why not?* Emily thought. *I've got all afternoon, and I want to
drive alongside the ocean.* She knew the peaceful drive would give her an
opportunity to think through everything Leigh Steinberg had shared
with her. *What a day!*

CHAPTER 7

GOOD MEDICINE:
BETH MCQUISTON

Emily could see that Beth McQuiston was a people person as soon as she entered the Abbott Senior Medical Director's third-floor office. Pictures of her daughter from babyhood through her teen years were scattered around the room, as were photos of co-workers and various items that McQuiston either had picked up on her travels or been given by people returning from *their* travels. A large L-shaped desk faced the door, and she also had a round table and chairs, enough for a group meeting, with a nearby whiteboard. A row of windows looked out over a pond with a fountain in its center.

McQuiston's office was in the corporate headquarters of Abbott's Diagnostic building north of Chicago, where she'd been a medical director in diagnostics for more than ten years. After college and graduate studies in food science, she'd worked as a dietitian for a few years. Then, at twenty-eight, McQuiston went back to school to take prerequisites for medical school and begin her journey to become a neurologist.

A thin, perky woman with long blond hair, McQuiston was drinking kombucha when Emily was ushered in.

"I'm happy to meet you, Dr. McQuiston," Emily said.

"Please call me Beth," McQuiston said. Holding up her cup, she asked, "Would you like me to get you one of these? Kombucha is great for your gut microbiome."

"No, thanks," Emily said.

She knew kombucha was good for you but found the taste disgusting. Her choice of fermented beverage was beer.

"How about some tea?" McQuiston asked.

"Sure," Emily said, relieved to get something somewhat more normal to drink.

"Green, white, black, decaf?"

"Um, green, with half a teaspoon of honey if possible."

"Nice!" McQuiston said approvingly. She left to go acquire the tea.

Upon her return she said, "You really have to be protective of your gut. A lot of your brain and how you feel starts with your gut. Even when I travel, I carry my vitamins and my fish oils and my turmeric, and as soon as I get in my rental car, I buy kombucha and put it in the fridge in my hotel room."

"Sounds like you're very aware of what you eat and drink," Emily said.

"Absolutely. I'm a vegetarian, except for the fish oils. I have a banana every day, for the potassium. Even at Disney World, we make healthy choices, like mango slices instead of candy or hot dogs."

"I guess you never stop being a nutritionist," Emily said.

"Well, that was my first love," McQuiston said. "I studied food science, got my graduate degree, and spent several years working in nutrition. Then I got interested in research, and that got me into renal nutrition, which is nutrition affecting the kidneys. My first mentor was Jordi Goldstein-Fuchs, who was editor of the *Journal of Renal Nutrition*. She liked a piece I sent in for publication, and I wound up writing several chapters of a book with her. I was just in my twenties then and working on a book!

"It was a pivotal experience for me. Jordi reached out and said, 'Hey, I see potential in you, and I think you would be really good at writing about nutrition.' And she was right! I was good at it and enjoyed it. I started publishing a lot of different things in journals about nutrition because Jordi gave of her time and insights. She didn't have to reach out to me, but she did. I became an assistant editor of the journal, which was an amazing experience.

"During that time, I had friends who were doctors, and I started learning from them about what they did. I read books like *Harrison's Principles of Internal Medicine* for fun at home, and one day Jordi said to me, 'You know, you can do this in real life if you want to.' And my twin sister said, 'You should just do this because you love it.' Suddenly all my friends were encouraging me to go to med school. So I went, and I loved it, took to it like a duck to water."

"According to Don, you love mentoring, and it's big in your network," Emily said.

"I love Don. Please say hi to him for me!" McQuiston said. "And yes, definitely. It's unfortunate, in this day and age, that girls and women are still a minority in science fields traditionally dominated by men. So many girls are still told what their roles in the workplace can be. But you don't know until you try different things if it's going to be the thing you love. It's all about exposing people to different areas, getting kids in front of every opportunity, because you don't know what's going to click for them and what their passion is going to be.

"And for many of us, it's science. Science is everywhere," she continued. "Why does toast smell good? That's food science. How do you make lipstick that stays on? That's chemistry. How does my bike work? That's physics. And when you have an opportunity to put a kid in front of science, you grab it. When I had to have an air conditioner replaced, I had my daughter shadow the gentleman installing it, and he showed her how compressors and condensers work. You go to relatives, friends, neighbors, and ask, 'Hey, would you mind talking to my daughter about what you do?' They find out that science is exciting and relatable."

Emily smiled to herself, thinking about all the vacations when her family would go to the pool or out to the beach, and she'd stay behind to ask questions of the people who worked there. "What happens if somebody staying at the hotel gets really sick?" "Who decides how much the stuff in the vending machine costs?" "Have you ever had to call the police to come here?" *Boy, was I a pest*, she thought.

"I always tell young women, 'If you don't ask, you don't get, so try to get as many exposures as you can,'" McQuiston said. "And I tell parents to encourage their kids. Yeah, there might be setbacks; nobody gets it 100 percent out of the gate. One of the best things a parent or a teacher or really any mentor can do is say, 'Okay. Maybe you didn't get that, but it was a learning experience, and keep going.' It's not always about being the smartest or the best. It's about grit, it's about determination, and it's about passion. If you have those, you absolutely will succeed in business. Succeeding in life is a bit more complicated."

"I'll tell you this too: the benefit goes both ways."

"How many young women have you mentored over the years?" Emily asked.

"Oh, I can't think of a number right now, but dozens and dozens," McQuiston replied. "Abbott started mentoring programs years ago.

The high school intern program has been around since 2012. Most of the interns are from backgrounds that are underrepresented in STEM careers, and more than half are young women. We have interns at Abbott locations around the world. Ninety percent of them pursue STEM majors in college.

"I'll tell you this too: the benefit goes both ways. We mentor and train and expose these bright minds to many different areas of science, but these kids also bring phenomenal positive energy to us. I had one intern working on global neuroscience translational research, and she brought a lot of vibrancy to the team. We all worked really well together. After she left to return to college, she brought that training forward to the world and is now developing a methodology to collect cerebral spinal fluid from patients to make this experience more comfortable for them."

"That's amazing," Emily said.

McQuiston continued, "And I want the girls to pay it forward, so now when I'm someone's mentor, I have her become a mentor too. That's when you really see someone light up, when you ask *her* to mentor another girl. This is about succeeding in life, not just business.

"One year, I had a college STEM intern and a high school STEM intern, so I had the college intern mentor the high school intern. We mentored both of them, of course, but the college student helping the high school student meant she was giving back. We help you, then you help someone else and continue the chain. When the college intern mentored the high school intern, they loved it; it was profoundly impactful for both of them. They both said at the end of the summer that it was one of the most meaningful things they did. Success in life is about meaning!

"Are you familiar with eudemonic happiness? I think you'll enjoy reading about it," she said and smiled.

"Will do. I take it you've had mentors since Dr. Goldstein-Fuchs," Emily said.

"Goodness, yes. I had a lot of help when I started medical school. I was a nontraditional student in that I was getting close to thirty and not right out of college, but the school, Rush University in Chicago, was very generous to me. Then, too, medical school repeatedly presents a microcosm of the whole mentoring process. For every procedure, you're told, 'See one, do one, teach one.' You learn from the people ahead of you, and once you've mastered the procedure, you're expected to pass on your ability to someone else. This formula teaches much more than just the procedures.

"The medical college at Rush has a long history of volunteerism too. There were a bunch of ways you could help the local community, which was underserved in health services. In fact, you could do rotations in community clinics. Or you could volunteer at a shelter, or help plan a fundraiser, or work with kids in the community. We also had a program every year for premed college students where they could shadow med students and find out what the medical school experience was like."

"Where did your interest in mentoring and volunteerism come from?"

"I went to schools that focused on giving," McQuiston said. "Even when I was very young, community service was considered important, so I was always riding my bike raising money for a charity. There were blanket drives and food drives and clothing drives, you name it. When I was in high school, you could volunteer at the local orphanage or the nursing home and for Special Olympics. I was always volunteering for different things and actually never gave it a thought; it just became part of who I am."

"So, Beth, can we talk about the science of generosity?" Emily asked. "I've read one article after another about how generosity makes you feel good. Is there a measurable scientific aspect to that?"

"Absolutely," McQuiston said confidently. "Science can't explain everything, and some of the evidence is anecdotal, but there are enough studies to provide a scientific basis that generosity feels good to the body, not just the soul, and that human beings and a lot of other animal species are generous by nature.

> **"Being generous has been a survival mechanism of human beings."**

"Over the millennia, being generous has been a survival mechanism of human beings. We've been around this long because our ancestors discovered that working in collaboration with others served them much better than 'every man for himself.' People found out that sharing food and living space, and working together to grow and find food and to build shelter—what we call prosocial behavior—helped everybody in a community have access to food and shelter and kept most people alive long enough to produce another generation. Prosocial behavior may in fact be an evolutionary adaptation that has promoted the survival of our species as well as other animal species."

"That's fascinating and logical, but how does it relate to how we feel today when we do something generous?" Emily asked.

"Great question. Over time, the pull toward sharing and collaborating on the practical level evolved into something that actually affected our brain chemistry. We have been developed, become designed in a way that we get a boost from being generous," McQuiston said. "And if generosity produces pleasurable feelings, it makes people more likely to do it again, and they continue the cycle.

"Generosity actually impacts your brain's reward circuits. We see this on functional imaging—brain scans. Different areas of the brain that are metabolically active when you do something light up. Doctors have seen that the mesolimbic reward system, which is activated by stimuli like sex, drugs, food, and receiving money, lights up when you are generous. One study found that when one person decided to share something equitably with another person, it activated the orbitofrontal cortex, suggesting that people feel good when they ensure equity, even when that fairness comes at a personal cost."

> "Generosity actually impacts your
> brain's reward circuits."

"What brain chemicals or hormones are involved?"

"Well, there's dopamine, which is the neurotransmitter produced when you're doing something you love. It spikes when you do something generous, even if it's just smiling at someone or giving a compliment, and you just feel good. That's good for whomever you are helping, and it encourages you to do it again, because you want that dopamine rush again.

"The other chemical most folks associate with generosity is oxytocin, which has a reputation as the 'love hormone.' It's a messenger for sexual arousal, romantic attachment, and bonding behavior. Oxytocin gets released when you exhibit empathy, when you give to charity, when you help someone out. Oxytocin also has an effect on sociability and on trust: it helps a person trust others without being gullible.

"People even feel the effect of oxytocin when they *witness* an act of kindness. One study found that participants who watched a video clip of musicians thanking their former teachers were more likely to volunteer for an unpaid study or spend time helping with a tedious task, compared to people who watched a funny video or one that didn't call for any response.

"Then there's serotonin, which keeps you in a good mood, and endorphins, which are natural painkillers, the source of the 'runner's high' that outweighs any discomfort a runner feels. Endorphins that are triggered by an act of generosity can have a similar effect, a 'helper's high.' And vasopressin, which is similar to oxytocin in structure. It mostly regulates kidney function and how often you pee, but it also influences feelings of closeness and compassion."

"Wow. The fact there is real science behind this connection between generosity and human relationships is amazing. What else have scientists found out about generosity?" Emily asked enthusiastically.

"They've run studies showing that people are more generous when they feel more connected to others. For example, one study found that when people were primed with words that implied relatedness, like *community, together, and relationship,* they later showed a greater interest in volunteering and donated significantly more to charity than people who were primed with neutral words. The same study also found that people reported a stronger intention to act generously in the future after writing about a time when they felt a strong bond with someone else."

"That makes people sound awfully impressionable or suggestible."

"Oh, not really," McQuiston said. "Not everyone is the same. The kind of prosocial empathy that gives people the potential to be generous is present in different amounts in different people. Some people are naturally highly altruistic, but others are less inclined toward trust or acts of selflessness."

"How does that play out in the workplace?" Emily asked.

"The science on that is pretty clear. Leaders who are compassionate toward their employees, as shown by neuroimaging research, cause those employees' brains to respond more positively. Creating a culture of generosity has been linked with lower emotional exhaustion among employees and lower absenteeism. Employees stay at their jobs when they have a sense of belonging and being valued; they're more likely to quit when their work relationships are mainly transactional.

"Numerous studies show that when leaders are less focused on being 'in charge' and more focused on the well-being of their employees, that's a strong predictor of job satisfaction, perceived organizational support, loyalty to and trust in the organization, and retention. Such an attitude is linked to better motivation to improve one's job performance and also has been linked to better team performance. Generosity often is considered a 'soft skill,' but there is empirical evidence that compassion for employees is beneficial not just for those employees but for the boss. If you look up servant leadership, there are many articles and books written on why it's so powerful.

"One longitudinal study used validated research scales to assess the personality traits of people entering the labor market. After fourteen years, controlling for demographic and corporate factors, those who were selfish, aggressive, and manipulative were less likely to move up the ranks. Instead, those who were generous and agreeable were more likely to be promoted to a position of leadership. Another study that included a wide range of income levels found that people with prosocial motivation have higher incomes compared to selfish people. I wish more people just coming into the workplace understood this instead of finding out about it when they're middle-aged."

> **"Those who were generous and agreeable were more likely to be promoted to a position of leadership."**

"I never knew that being kind gives you a better career than being tough," Emily marveled. "How do you make that kind of leadership the norm?"

"For one thing, parents need to nurture it, and they need to start when their kids are very young. Generosity starts before many kids can talk," McQuiston said.

"Many studies show toddlers between one and three years old helping both peers and adults with problems the toddlers themselves perceive. A study of eighteen- and thirty-month-old children found that at both ages, toddlers voluntarily engaged in instrumental helping, like handing an adult a clothespin that is out of the adult's reach; empathic helping, giving a blanket to an adult who feels cold or a toy to someone who is sad; and altruistic helping, like when a child hands over their own blanket to a chilly adult or the child's favorite toy to a sad adult.

"Studies have also shown pairs of children eighteen to twenty-four months who will divide resources equally between themselves, even when one child has to sacrifice some of their own resources to ensure equality. Another found that toddlers will proactively help out after an accident, for example by picking up an object that someone else has dropped without noticing.

"Parents need to encourage children to be generous for the sake of generosity," McQuiston continued. "They don't need to bribe kids into those kinds of behaviors. In fact, children may be less inclined when generosity is transactional, like the mom who says, 'If you share with that other boy, I'll take you for ice cream later.' It's better for parents to raise young children to see helping as part of their identity and nurture empathy in their kids."

"That makes such perfect sense. Can adults who aren't naturally generous be persuaded it's the best way to be?" Emily asked.

"Sure," McQuiston said. "It can be socially contagious. A team of researchers found that a generous act by one person could inspire generosity in someone three degrees removed from them, showcasing how each person in a network can influence dozens or even hundreds of people. That's an upside of social media; it can make acts of kindness go viral. And in some cases it takes just one person to set the example— be an influencer, in today's usage.

"When you start a network of generosity like this, you're building systems in which to be generous. That's a scientific thing to do—scientists are always building systems. It's just amazing what happens when kindness goes viral. The effect is tremendous."

> "It can be socially contagious ... a generous act by one person could inspire generosity in someone three degrees removed."

Emily paused. What McQuiston just said was very powerful. The idea of creating networks of generosity and systematizing it was captivating.

"Next you're going to tell me it's as good as medicine."

"It is! Being generous absolutely has health benefits!" McQuiston said excitedly. "There's been a lot of research on this. Being a giving person who's focused on others is linked with longer life. Generosity can reduce high blood pressure and other risk factors for cardiovascular disease. It can decrease stress and accompanying levels of cortisol, the hormone most associated with stress, which in turn may lower blood sugar. Being generous may help people maintain vitality and cognitive function as they age, help alleviate symptoms of depression, and even relieve pain. It's all supported by research.

"It's true even for many older adults, the very people who tell us, 'Oh, I'm too old to change.' Volunteering is linked to greater quality of life, with one study reporting that frequent helpers reported feeling more vitality and self-esteem—but only if the volunteer work was something they chose and weren't dragged into.

"Another study found that among participants reporting low physical activity levels as the research began, those who volunteered increased their physical activity by an average of 110 percent, more than double, while non-volunteers increased their activity by just 12 percent. These results suggest that volunteering may be a good way to increase physical activity in older adults who are primarily inactive— and physical activity, of course, is linked to better health."

"That's pretty compelling evidence," Emily said.

"Yes, but scientific studies just put some numbers to what a lot of us have known for a long time: Being generous just plain and simple brings you joy," McQuiston said. "It helps you feel good and it helps other people feel good. It gives your life a sense of meaning. It helps you focus on what is important. And at the same time you're helping someone else, you're helping yourself too. Your attitude becomes more positive; you feel better about the future. If you need to lift your spirits, what's better for you, volunteering your time or eating a pint of ice cream out of the carton?"

Or maybe eating a croissant with a latte on the veranda, Emily thought.

"Giving promotes a sense of social connectedness," McQuiston continued. "It's not about giving money; it's about caregiving and helping others. It's the extra pot of that yummy soup you make to share with friends, co-workers, or neighbors. It's cutting an elderly neighbor's lawn or raking their leaves or shoveling their front walk. The key is that human connection.

"Of course, so many of us spend our time looking at our smartphones. That's a downside of social media: People think they're connecting with someone when they chat via text, but generosity toward individuals, especially people you know, is best done in person. It is really important to get together. Even if it means having to carve out time from a hectic schedule, that in-person connection is important. When you volunteer and you're with other people who want to help others, you are going to feel a sense of community, a sense of connectedness, a sense of feeling like you are doing something important in the world. You are going to feel really good."

"This is exciting stuff," Emily said. "An opportunity for everyone, it seems, if more people understood. But does it matter whether you know who's benefiting from your generosity?"

"I don't think so," McQuiston said. "Sometimes you know and sometimes you don't. Sometimes you don't even know if the generous thing you did had an effect. One night I was out at a restaurant, and this girl was sitting at another table crying. I went over and asked, 'Are you okay?' She told me she had just broken up with her boyfriend, and I gave her a hug, then I went back to my table. I hope knowing that I cared about her helped her feel a little better, but I'll probably never know.

"There's evidence that we derive more emotional benefits from generosity when we know the recipient than when we don't, but we still feel good even if our generosity extends to persons unknown, which is what happens when you donate to a charity or other nonprofit. You know your money will go to hungry people or children with cancer, but you don't know which individuals will benefit. We're the only species that gives to benefit people we don't know, but that doesn't take away the pleasure of doing it."

"It sounds as if there are unlimited ways to be generous."

"Definitely!" McQuiston said. The more she talked, the more animated she became. "It doesn't have to be about money. It doesn't even have to be about giving something tangible, like food. It can be a smile or a ride to a doctor's appointment or teaching someone how to fix a problem instead of scolding them for making a mistake. It could be a text to someone to say 'I'm thinking about you' or sharing a memory. Or verbally thanking a cashier, a receptionist, a server in a restaurant for doing a good job.

"I will say, it helps build generosity if you maintain a positive outlook on life. Our brains are good at finding the negative things, the risks, the problems. I encourage people to pay extra attention to the positive thoughts they have throughout the day and articulate them whenever they can. Something like, 'Hey, Steve, I thought your input on that project was really helpful, I appreciate that.' The appreciation part is very important; it's even more impactful than saying 'Thank you.' Telling someone you appreciate them and exactly what you appreciate can be life-changing."

"But there must be some people who can't let go of negativity," Emily said. "I've met people who think being positive makes you a pushover or a patsy." *Like me sometimes,* she thought. "Not everyone can look at the world through rose-colored glasses."

"Having a positive outlook isn't the same as wearing rose-colored glasses," McQuiston said. "If you look at the world through rose-colored glasses, you're seeing a distortion of reality. I'm talking about seeing the positive things that actually exist—the employee who goes above and beyond, the team that produces a great project—and celebrating them *out loud.*

"Plus I don't believe that most people who have made a habit of negativity have to stay that way," she continued. *"Change is possible—* there's research that proves it. All of us can become more generous if we are intentional about change. We are all works in progress, but if we believe we can get better at generosity, we will.

"That said, you're right, Emily, there are people who can't let go of negativity. You want to avoid them as much as you can. Some people just drain you because they're emotional vampires. They pull you down, put effort into making you unhappy. You try to help them have a lighter attitude, but nothing you do works. I learned back in med school, during my psychiatry rotation, that people make you feel how they feel. So you don't want to be around people like that—you want to be around people who make you feel good. Pick the people to be around that you aspire to be, the ones who make you feel good, the ones who volunteer their time, who are living their best life. Part of your self-care is to be aware of people who are toxic for you."

Emily thought, *Letting someone go who's negatively impacting others and won't consider changing is going to be important. To be generous with the team, you have to let the negative people go find a new place to be negative.*

"Speaking of self-care, Beth, how do you take care of yourself? Besides healthy eating?" Emily asked.

"Well, I get enough exercise," McQuiston said. "I take the stairs and not the elevator. I try to take a five-mile walk. I practice mindful meditation, and I make sure to get enough sleep.

"As a neuroscientist, I think it's important that you go outside for five to ten minutes within the first thirty minutes after you get up in the morning. You want to get exposure to natural light, even if it is overcast. It helps reset your circadian rhythm, helps your mental focus and balance, and it activates your happy, feel-good hormones."

"I've never heard that before," Emily said. "I have to try that."

"Basically, I am a million percent behind looking after yourself and being the best version of yourself that you can be," McQuiston said. "So one of my top priorities is to take care of my physical and mental well-being."

"Tell me more," Emily said.

"I pay attention to mental weeds, which is what I call negative thoughts. If some thoughts in my head are not helpful, I pull them out and try to reframe them in a helpful or more positive manner. I actually visualize myself pulling a weed out of my brain. Let's say I'm in traffic and the expressway is backed up for miles because there was an accident. I'm not going to get all worked up about it and worry that I'm going to be late to work. I reframe it and say to myself, *I hope everyone is all right. Thank God I wasn't in the accident.* Instead of stewing, I try to get rid of negative thoughts and see bad events as something I can use to think about gratitude and change."

I wonder if that works, thought Emily, veteran of many a traffic jam.

"Anything else?" she asked.

"Well, I pay attention to the beauty around me. If it's snowing, I think about how beautiful it looks coming down rather than how it's going to mess up traffic. I appreciate the leaves on trees coming out as tiny babies in the spring, then how the trees look in full leaf, and the lovely colors the leaves turn in the fall. When my daughter was small, I took her everywhere with me. I didn't want to miss a minute with her that I didn't have to, and I am continually appreciative that the places I worked let me do that.

"In general, I do the things I know I need to do to be the person I want to be. I make time every day for a tea break, and I make time to meet with friends or team members just to laugh and have a good time. When I suggest this to people and they say, 'I don't have time to do something like that,' I tell them, 'Well, you don't have time *not* to do it. How do you want to feel at the end of the day: droopy or happy?"

Okay, I was doing the daily latte break, Emily thought, *but I never had friends or co-workers I could laugh with. How much of that was my work situation, and how much was me?*

"The part of being generous that may seem counterintuitive is to be exactly who you are, to keep your priorities straight and put them first, before other people's priorities."

"The part of being generous that may seem counterintuitive is to be exactly who you are, to keep your priorities straight and put them first."

"To be authentic?" Emily asked.

"Yes, to be authentic," McQuiston said, nodding vigorously. "Remember, you're with yourself twenty-four hours a day, seven days a week. If someone is rude to you in a store, that person is with you for only thirty seconds. If you have to calm down an unruly meeting, those people are with you for an hour. But only you have to live with yourself 24/7.

"I used to consult an Olympic marathon gold medalist, and she's the one who told me, 'Run your own race. You can't keep tempo with the beat of someone else's drum.' You need to believe in yourself; what works for the next person may not work for you. And that goes back to being positive. If you get to the halfway point with a project, the idea is not to think, *Oh my God, that was like pulling teeth—what's the second half going to be like?* but rather, *Okay, we made it this far, we can handle the rest.* Make every challenge an opportunity."

"And you really think positivity and generosity will win the day?"

"I really do," McQuiston said. "You may have to be patient, but eventually they will pay off. They dampen that existentialist *angst* that's hard not to feel, and they give you a sense of purpose and serenity. You have the feeling that you are forging a legacy that other people will be happy to receive, and you'll leave the world a better place than you found it."

Emily thanked McQuiston and they exchanged pleasantries, then Emily headed out.

On the way back into Chicago, sure enough, Emily got caught in stop-and-go traffic on the expressway. The electric sign above the road read "BACK UP 3 MILES TO DEERFLD RD/2 LT LNS CLOSED/ ROAD WORK." Emily sighed. She hated sitting in traffic and dreaded the bottleneck. Then she remembered what McQuiston had said about pulling mental weeds. *I'm not in a hurry,* she thought. *Whatever they're doing up ahead, the road will wind up better for the commuters. This car has Sirius XM.*

Emily smiled and reached over to turn on the radio. *Think I'll just take my time. That's what Beth would do, isn't it?!*

As the music washed over her, she reflected on the plane ride ahead, and the two days of rest and reflection she would have, the opportunity to enjoy herself at home before her next interview. Instead of bemoaning the lines she'd face at the airport and the journey home, she pulled up those mental weeds, focusing on all the opportunities for kindness.

I can thank the airline staff for helping me to get home. I can be gracious to the TSA agents for keeping me and the other passengers safe. Like Beth, I can choose to be grateful.

Ahead of Emily, the traffic started to shift, and her car, along with all of the others, moved on.

CHAPTER 8

HERE FOR EACH OTHER: JACK PANNELL

Driving through Columbus, Emily took in the leafy trees and eclectic architecture outside of her rental car. A mix of older art deco-style buildings and sleek, newer towers whizzed by as she drove on to meet Jack Pannell. Rolling down the window and breathing in the clean air, she could see why he lived in Ohio. It felt so tranquil, even welcoming. Pulling up to his address, she brushed off her jacket, walked up, and knocked on the door.

Pannell opened his front door and ushered Emily in. He was a smiling, fit man in his sixties and immediately put Emily at ease. She smiled back, reflecting Pannell's geniality.

"Hello!" he said. "You must be Emily Gardner. Please call me Jack."

He got her seated in a comfortable club chair and sat on the sofa.

"Now tell me more about this project you're doing," he continued. "All I know is that you're researching generosity and Don thinks there can be more of it at Pinafore."

"Yes, that's the main idea," Emily said.

"You don't think the people are generous now?" Pannell asked.

"Great question, I think a lot of us have a strong desire to be generous, but we don't necessarily understand what generosity really is or how to implement it," Emily admitted. "Some went to high schools with a community-service requirement, or they were involved in social justice work while in college, others constantly do acts of kindness, but they don't consider these to be generosity. They think of it as giving money or stuff, confusing it with financial philanthropy."

"You're right, and that's not enough," Pannell said. "It's hard for many to understand the difference between financial philanthropy and generosity in the broader sense. When they give their time and energy to projects that help nonprofit organizations or help people directly, they're being generous, but they don't realize it's much more than that.

"Generosity involves humility, mentoring, not stepping on someone else to get ahead," he continued. "It's being nice to someone even if it's Monday and you're in a bad mood, smiling and showing a new hire around the office when you have a pile of work on your desk. Basically, it's doing good things just because it's the right thing to do. But it makes you happy and benefits you in unexpected ways."

"I guess so," Emily said with a smile. "And Don said you're an example of someone who makes a point of being generous by that definition."

"Oh, man," Pannell said. "Don is always using me as an example of something. We went to high school together, and he's probably forgotten a lot of the trouble we used to get into."

"Trouble?" Emily said, her eyebrows raised. Don was always wrapped up so tight!

"Nothing serious," Pannell said, but there was a twinkle in his eye. "Anyway, that's a story for another day."

"Of course," Emily said, still marveling that Don could have been any shade of a troublemaker as a youngster. She always pictured him as the kind of kid who kept his head down, followed all the rules, got all As, and graduated class valedictorian.

"Let's start at the beginning," she said. "What was your upbringing like?"

"Well, let's see," Pannell mused. "I grew up right here in Ohio. Four generations of my family still live within a mile of each other. I thought it was mighty slow when I was eighteen, and I couldn't wait to leave, but as an adult, I've come back several times to reflect and recharge before the next chapter of my life.

"Our home, when I was growing up, was always open to friends and strangers. You never knew who was going to be at the dinner table. My dad or mom would meet someone on the street and invite them over for dinner. We never had dinner in front of the TV, because dinner was a time to engage and have conversations about anything and everything. My mom and dad set a great example for me.

"I did go to college in the Northeast and have done most of my work on the East Coast, but I have to say, I think people in the Midwest are a little kinder and less superficial than folks who live on the East Coast. No one in Ohio asks me where I went to school or what I do for a living. I have these fresh, wonderful encounters with people exactly where they are. And people are so kind—you know, I see them go out of their way to be kind."

"Can you give me an example?"

"Sure. Not long ago on a really cold day, I had to put air in one of my tires. I was going to do it myself at a gas station, but my sister said I should just go to the Jiffy Lube and knock on the door, and someone will come out and put air in my tire. 'Do I have to pay him for it?' I asked her. 'No,' my sister said, 'just knock on the door.'

"I didn't believe her, but I went to Jiffy Lube and asked the kid behind the counter if anyone could help me put some air in a tire. The kid said, 'Sure, I can do that.' He came out and put air in the tire, twenty degrees, no gloves. He wouldn't even let me give him a tip. You don't necessarily find that kind of kindness on the East Coast."

"That's true," Emily said.

"It's an example of something I was taught as a boy and have been reminded of all my life: We are not put on this planet to be here for ourselves. If we were, if that were the plan for all of us, I think the world would be a pretty miserable place. Instead, I think we get an opportunity to be helpful every day. We have a chance to get out of ourselves and help someone whom we just happen to meet. That person can be a co-worker, a family member, the guy at Jiffy Lube, a kid running the streets. We have opportunities every day to be generous with or helpful to the next guy.

> **"We are not put on this planet to be here for ourselves."**

"I was lucky that at my first job, we were not only encouraged but *required* to demonstrate what they called spirit of service. In fact, we were graded on it! I never knew exactly what rubric they used for that, how they figured out how kind you were, but I knew intuitively that it meant the amount of service you provided to people and the genuine interest you had in other people."

"Tell me more about your parents," Emily said.

"My dad was born in 1913 to an impoverished family in Virginia, and he went to work in the local coal mines when he was probably twelve or fourteen years old. For many years I thought he was hard on me, but at the same time he was loving toward and genuinely interested in other people. But later I realized he was raising me to live up to a very high standard of conduct. No matter where we went—and we traveled a lot when I was a kid—my father within seconds would be talking to a stranger on the street or someone working in a hotel. He had an intuitive sense about how he could be helpful to people. Today we would say he had high emotional intelligence.

"My father was helpful to people in so many ways. He was the guy you would call in our community if your son got in trouble in the middle of the night for a prank, like stealing someone's tires. We would get a call at two in the morning saying, 'Mr. Pannell, my son is in jail. Can you help?' And my father would say, 'I'll be right there.' He wasn't a minister, or a lawyer, or someone who sat on the city council, but everybody knew that he could help people fix their problems. I observed that my whole life.

"You also have to let people help *you*," Pannell said. "Let people be generous on your behalf. Whether it's about school, business, or the community where you live, it has been my experience that once I allow myself to be helped or even ask for help, doors seem to open for me in a way I'm not sure they open for other people who try to go it alone. It can be intimidating because you are being vulnerable, but I think we exist in order to be here for each other. It takes a certain confidence to both be kind and to accept kindness.

"A big part of that is the teacher-student or mentor-neophyte relationship. If you're just learning, you have the responsibility to expand your skills as much as you can, and you can't really do that by yourself. And if you already have the knowledge or skills, it's your responsibility to teach them to anyone who really wants to learn them."

"Who were some of your teachers?" Emily asked, thinking of Don. *I couldn't have wished for a better mentor*, she thought.

"I've had some great teachers and mentors, and not just early in my career. One of my first bosses, a man I've stayed in touch with, introduced me to Rick Woolworth. Rick worked in the investment bank where I had my first job out of college. But we met much later in life, when he had retired. He really was all about mentorship; he started an organization called Telemachus that was focused on intergenerational relations and wrote articles about mentorship. Rick and I were introduced via Zoom and started talking during Covid. We would have a phone call every two weeks, and I got to see up close a remarkable man who was phenomenal in his ability to connect with people. He would say that his job was to help people grow fruit on other people's trees, however he could.

"Rick was an expert networker. Hundreds, if not thousands, of people in every field were just a phone call away. If you had a problem or a question, or you needed a favor, he would pick up the phone and make happen whatever it was that needed to happen. His network was a result of his kindness and yet truly a tremendous asset. Rick was an important mentor with a wonderful, generous spirit. Unfortunately, he died suddenly of an aortic dissection at age sixty-nine, a shock to everyone, because he had been completely healthy up to that point. There must have been seven or eight hundred people at his memorial service, because he was one of the most-loved and, yes, generous people in the business community."

"Wow," Emily said. "I understand you also worked for the late Representative John Lewis."

"Yes, what a great opportunity to get to work for a civil rights hero. I was working as a press secretary in the political world, and the chance just fell in my path. At some point someone who knew Lewis said to me, 'Jack, you should go meet with John Lewis. I think you guys would be wonderful working with each other.' The next thing I knew, I was sitting down with one of the major figures of the civil rights movement. We talked for what seemed like two or three hours, and at the end of our conversation, Lewis said that he'd like me to come onto his team. We got up and hugged each other. There are people I feel an instant connection with, as if they were my brother or sister, and I will just hug them and say 'Thank you.' That's what happened with John Lewis."

"How did you get into your current career, building and running schools?"

"I chased fame and fortune in three careers: the Wall Street investment banking world, the entertainment business, and politics. I was working for the mayor of Washington, DC, and had a comfortable existence, and then I had the opportunity to meet a young man through a program called Abused and Neglected Children, which helps children in the family system. The program seeks to help the family stabilize itself during challenges and keep itself together rather than putting kids into foster homes.

"I became a court-appointed advocate for this young man who was about to be removed from his family. The advocate works as the eyes and ears of the court, reporting back on how their particular assigned child is doing, so I got involved with the young man's life. He was one of three children his blind grandmother was caring for, and I was supposed to report on whether the grandmother was up to the job of mothering her grandchildren.

"One day she asked me if I could go up to her grandson's school to check in on him. I went to the school and was appalled by what was going on in the school, a public school in Washington, DC. Now, I had gone to public schools. In fact, I was one of the kids who desegregated a public school in Dayton, Ohio. But by comparison, the school I saw that day was a trash pit, with overcrowded classrooms, outdated textbooks, and unruly students. Few kids could really learn there. That experience changed everything. From that day onward, I asked myself, 'What can I do to make a difference in educating these children—particularly those boys and young men of color that I deeply related to?' That led to 'What am I doing with my life?' and 'What should I be doing with my life?' It was the first time that I actually thought of education in terms of a career for myself."

"As Don would say, 'Who do you want to be?'" Emily mused. "It sounds like you acted on those questions."

"Yes," Pannell said. "I grew up in a family of service, a family that made a difference in the lives of many people, but that wasn't my life until the moment I decided to be at the center of something that could make a difference. That's when I set upon the journey to create a school, an all-boys school in Baltimore, where almost 80 percent of Black boys in fourth grade couldn't read at grade level. At that time, I didn't know a lot about education or the business of education. I learned about education from the ground up by asking hundreds of people how education could become better. What needed to be done, and how should we do it? It was a daunting endeavor.

"After several years of research, we got to the business of creating an application to establish a charter school, the Baltimore Collegiate School for Boys. We were approved and opened our doors in 2015 to 175 boys, grades four through eight. Before long, the school grew to five hundred boys, with another five hundred families on the waiting list. Something that started on my kitchen table became a source of good for almost a thousand families in Baltimore, because their sons had an opportunity to experience a great education, and through that education find and discover who they were and who they could become. Opening a school in Baltimore in 2015 was the hardest work at the hardest possible time, as America awakened to the facts of systematic racial discrimination and poor education."

"Why a single-sex school?" Emily asked.

"We designed Baltimore Collegiate," Pannell explained, "as an all-boys school because it encourages boys to see themselves as academically capable, which is important especially during the middle-school years. Research shows that boys' schools do a better job of recognizing and addressing the developmental needs of boys and encouraging their creativity, along with promoting academic achievement. Our choices show up especially well in our very successful sports program. Since 2015, our teams have won ten middle-school championships.

"There's a large emphasis on character as well: the qualities that we value and practice are integrity, wisdom, courage, compassion, and resilience," he continued. "We strive to develop critical-thinking skills, clear communication, problem-solving abilities, and a sense of agency in the boys' actions. Men and boys are in profound trouble in our society. Regardless of race and socioeconomic class, more and more young men are not entering the world of work and finding meaningful work. One in four young men report they have no close friends. Let me repeat that, *one in four young men say they have no close friends.* This is tragic!

"Baltimore Collegiate has given me a mission: making high-quality education accessible to as many people as possible, because so many people have limited educational opportunities and, later, job opportunities. I stepped down recently from leadership of Baltimore Collegiate and am working on establishing an all-boys charter school in Philadelphia and a faith-based prep school for boys in Phoenix. In addition, I founded an organization called The National Collegiate Academies, which has been invited to explore expansion of the Collegiate model for boys in Indianapolis, Nashville, Milwaukee, and Jacksonville."

"That's a tall order, to bring about a change in worldview, really, over a large geographical area," Emily said.

"It is, but it's possible," Pannell replied. "I think you can teach service to others—the Jesuits have been doing a good job with that for decades.

At Baltimore Collegiate, the boys recite a motto every day: 'Whatever hurts my brother, hurts me; whatever helps my brother, helps me.' That motto represents a way of living, and, with repetition, it sinks into the kids that it can be *their* way of living. They realize, 'I don't exist solely for myself and my desires and my needs. I exist to help others, to be of service to other people.' We've made our mission theirs. We've also taught our mission to more than 120 recent college graduates through our Collegiate Teaching Fellowships.

"Many boys come to us not knowing how to do things for themselves, let alone others. I will ask a boy, 'Do you make your bed? Do you feel that you have a responsibility in your home to make your bed every day?' A lot of them don't. They feel, *It's my bed, and whether I make it or don't make it doesn't affect anybody else.* They think of themselves as living life separately from others.

"People who share tight living space know better. Military recruits make their beds and keep their space tidy. So do kids who go to summer camp. We think of life as life together rather than life apart; the spirit changes when we think about life together in our community. So at Baltimore Collegiate, if there is a piece of trash on the floor, you're expected not to walk by it but to pick up the trash and throw it away properly—even if no one sees you do it."

> **"We think of life as life together rather than life apart."**

"And that happens?" Emily marveled. "Boys pick up trash they didn't drop?"

"They do," Pannell said. "All of us who are educators—and that includes not just teachers but administrators, parents, coaches—have daily, even hourly opportunities to impress upon young minds what it means for us to live in a good society together. You can have all the brain power in the world, but if you are not a decent human being, what difference are you going to make in society?"

"Indeed," Emily said. "Tell me this: How do you take care of yourself so that you have the energy to shape these young lives?"

"Good question," Pannell said. "I think of it as 'How do you care for your soul?' One important way is to give yourself some breathing room—literally.

"A few years ago, I woke up in the middle of the night and couldn't breathe. It stressed me out so much that I went to the emergency room. My blood pressure, they found out, was extremely high, so they did more tests, and at four in the morning a doctor said they were going to keep me in the hospital under observation for the next twenty-four hours. I had never been in the hospital overnight, so that took me aback. I was trying to beat my father's record; he lived to be ninety-five years old and never spent a night in the hospital until he was about eighty-six.

"The next morning, I called my assistant and asked them to bring my computer to the hospital but not to tell anyone I was there. The word must have gotten out, though, and after I got home, many friends wrote me notes and sent letters saying, 'I hear you were in the hospital. Are you okay?' They also reminded me that I couldn't do any good in the world if I were dead.

"That episode was a wake-up call," Pannell said. "I realized I had to slow down, take care of myself, be kind to myself. I didn't have to be at a thousand places at once, and I could say "no" once in a while. Now I schedule a quiet period of prayer and meditation from the time I get up to a good thirty minutes into my day. The days I don't do that, I feel it. My recommendation to you would be to teach people to do this starting much younger in life."

Good idea, Emily thought. "You referred earlier to a school in DC that was a real pit, and how you created the charter school so that some boys would have an alternative," she said. "What else do you see that can be fixed in a broken world?"

"Another good question," Pannell said. "I think there is a spiritual crisis afoot in this country. *The Wall Street Journal* published an article about this recently. I'm not sure it can be fixed, but I think it can be modified for the good, and we certainly have to address it. Many of us in leadership have sold people a few lies, and we have to unspin those lies. One of the lies is this notion that life is linear, running along a track, and every so often you get to a golden bell. If you hit the golden bell, you keep going down the track, you keep working hard and following the rules, and after you hit the last golden bell, you'll be happy. But life doesn't happen that way. You can tap all the golden bells and still wind up miserable. You can watch people take very different paths and see them end up on top of the world. We have to educate people that personal and professional fulfillment are intertwined zigzags rather than straight lines.

"We need to reeducate people, especially men, that being 'busy' is not the same as being successful, and we must, *must*, encourage men to loosen their biases. We are taught at a very early age to be tough, don't tell people you are hurting financially or mentally or emotionally, don't share your vulnerabilities with anyone except a professional—that is, if you or your cohort doesn't consider consulting a professional to be weakness. We live in a country where a bunch of men, including young Black men, are just bottled up. They don't know who they are, and no one knows who they are.

"At the same time, I think we have gotten to a state in the world where people are extremely self-focused. I call myself a naive pragmatist: I know how the world works, but I assume the best in everyone. I believe people are good. I'm always surprised when someone does something crooked or completely self-serving or unworthy of the person I know. People want to be good and do good, but they can lose direction. We need to still believe in them and help them get back on track.

"We also, I think, need to learn how to bring a light touch to life and not take ourselves too darn seriously. That could spare us a lot of over-reaction and self-centered focus and stress."

"What else should people be doing?"

"Part of successful living is to know who you are and feel really understood," Pannell said. "That comes more easily if you have people in your life who are willing to share their lives and thoughts with you and whom you trust enough to share with them. I have no fewer than five men in my life who can tell me anything and everything, and I can tell them anything and everything. I have to work at those relationships, but they are authentic, deep, and soulful. I would be surprised if any of the men in those circles would suddenly come upon a crisis that I wouldn't be aware of. These relationships are very important to my emotional well-being.

"This may seem trivial in comparison, but I also think the world would be a nicer place if everyone practiced good manners," Pannell said with a smile. "Once in an airport, one of the flight staff was trying to be helpful to everyone as we were waiting to take off. I observed how many passengers didn't say 'Thank you' as the flight attendant was helping put bags into the overhead bin, showing a kid how to buckle their seat belt, running around getting things for people and answering questions, finding people's seats, doing their job, always with a smile. That flight attendant deserved one 'Thank you' after another and barely got any. Saying 'Thank you,' even when you don't feel very thankful, is a little bit of the grease that helps the world run smoothly. Showing gratitude, to me, is such a simple form of generosity. It can make all the difference in that person's day.

> **"Showing gratitude, to me, is such
> a simple form of generosity."**

"It's important to be grateful. In fact, I make a gratitude list every night, and sometimes I will list what I am most grateful for and what I am least grateful for. And if thinking about the things you're least grateful for is like revisiting a sucker punch, that's all right, because you learned something from the experience, right? That's why it's on your 'least grateful' list, not an 'ungrateful' list. Even if I struggle to find a reason for gratitude, I know it happened for a reason, and the reason probably means that I'm annoyed with someone or even myself. Without gratitude, the rest doesn't work."

"We have so many opportunities to make mistakes," Emily said. "How do we undo consequences, learn from mistakes, and take them in stride? Isn't this part of being generous with ourselves?"

"Yes. First, there are no mistakes, only lessons," Pannell said. "The trick is to be awake and aware for the lesson. Consult other people—have the courage to say, 'This is what I did and how I did it. What could or should I have done differently?' I tell young people, particularly twentysomethings, that you're told not to make mistakes, but unless you are a surgeon, your best lessons, your best teachers, are mistakes.

"In fact, when I'm in a hiring position, I tell candidates, 'I don't want to hear about your successes; I want to hear about the three biggest mistakes you've made in life.' I'm always surprised that people are surprised by that question.

"But there is no better book than someone else's experience. And the funny thing is that most people can tell me their three biggest mistakes pretty easily. They come up with their mistakes more easily than they recount their successes. If you would ask me about three mistakes I've made in the work I'm doing, I can tell you without thinking hard about it: I over-trust people. Sometimes I move too fast, I'm too hasty. And sometimes I don't ask the right questions, so some hiccup will happen. By knowing my mistakes, I begin to understand them and avoid them. If I continue to make mistakes and don't change what I'm doing, then I'm not a learner, and I want to be a *constant* learner."

After some talk about the local sports teams and the wild weather in the Midwest, Emily thanked Pannell. "You've given me a lot to think about, just as Don said you would."

Emily walked slowly back to her rental car wondering about Jack Pannell's many careers and whether he thought the charter school venture was his last one. She wondered whether she was learning from her own mistakes and if she said "Thank you" enough. She wondered what traffic would be like going back to the airport. Most of all, she wondered what Don Jenkins possibly could have done as a teenager that would get him into trouble.

CHAPTER 9

CAPITAL IDEAS: SHERRIE BECKSTEAD

After an uneventful flight from the Midwest, Emily made her first stop on the East Coast, admiring the professional ease with which Washingtonians traversed the airport as though it was a normal stop on the daily commute. She was relieved she had been given twenty-four hours in Washington, DC, before her next meeting and was in no rush to be anywhere. Emily used the time to do some more research and walk a bit of the nation's capital. It was a little overwhelming when she stopped to look at a map and realized the Smithsonian Institution alone had nineteen museums, plus the zoo. And the National Mall connected almost every important building in the three branches of government, and more monuments and memorials than she could count. Where did one even begin? It reminded her of how she felt when she embarked on this journey just over a month ago.

The next afternoon Emily entered the lobby of the Willard InterContinental Hotel, not wanting to be a minute late for her appointment with Sherrie Beckstead. She was awestruck by the lushness and beauty of the lobby. Everything recalled a different century: the potted palms, the cream-colored marble columns with three-tiered bronze-colored capitals, the ornate divided ceiling, the rugs, the furniture, the light fixtures—all evoked an earlier, more gracious time. Emily was used to the sleek, unadorned luxury of Pinafore Global hotels and the utilitarian atmosphere of other hotel lobbies. Within seconds she could feel the history and weight of this building's presence.

Coming back to reality, Emily asked the concierge where afternoon tea was served and was directed to Peacock Alley; she was just in time for the second seating. She entered a lovely space full of tables set with exquisite, flower-sprigged china.

Emily saw Sherrie Beckstead seated, easy to recognize from photos she'd found online; the executive, leader, and philanthropist had been featured in what seemed like every magazine you can imagine for her acts and involvement.

"I'm so glad you had time to meet with me, Ms. Beckstead," Emily said as she approached the table and pulled out her chair.

"Please, call me Sherrie," Beckstead said. For her part, Emily was slightly intimidated by the elegant woman seated across from her, but that dissipated quickly. She could easily understand why Beckstead and Don were good friends. Like Don, Beckstead had that immediate calming presence of someone who knows exactly who they are and accepts you for exactly who you are. Emily aspired to many things; to have the confidence, style, and poise of her lunch date was one of them.

"What a lovely hotel this is," Emily said.

"I love it," Beckstead said. "I take a lot of my meetings in this space."

"I can see why," Emily said. "I feel special just sitting here."

"It's much nicer than any conference room or traditional office space in the DMV," Beckstead said. She ordered a formal tea for two. "So, Don didn't give me a lot to go on. What would you like to know?"

"Well, I've been tasked with learning about the power and influence of generosity. You are well known for being generous and supporting efforts and people you believe in," Emily said. "Can you tell me a little about how you came to earn that reputation? What informs your generosity?"

"Certainly my faith," Beckstead said confidently. "It's the epicenter of my life. It motivates and inspires me. Faith in God is something I worry many younger people today are missing. It ties in with our self-confidence, trust, and relationships, because if we don't believe in something greater than ourselves, we don't have the confidence to put down roots, reach out to others, deal with troubled times, or revel in good times."

Emily thought to herself, *I have faith, but when was the last time it directly influenced my actions?*

"Faith gives me the energy to embark on new projects," Beckstead continued. "I pray about it and put it out to the universe. Waking in the morning and watching the sun always instills a directional notion that I feel. I instinctively know if I should be involved in a project, if I have the energy and creativity that will be necessary. Prayer and meditation help me discern if next steps are a fit. My faith blossomed as a child and was the beacon of hope that sustained me through my husband's illness and eventual death. I really believe that faith is what brings about joy and confidence and allows us to be fulfilled as human beings."

> **"I really believe that faith is what brings about joy and confidence and allows us to be fulfilled as human beings."**

"Do you think generosity is a characteristic within us, like faith is, or is it more external, like taking an action or making a decision?" Emily asked.

"Both!" Beckstead said enthusiastically. "It's everything from serving on committees and boards to helping build a house to advocating for the rights of others. All of this must come from within, as does faith. It has to be intentional, and you have to take it personally. Maybe you could call it *heart*."

Emily stayed quiet, feeling the pause was a reflective moment for both.

"Sometimes I don't think we recognize our heart fully until we experience pain," Beckstead said, a bit quieter now. "I've known a dear friend who lost two children; I can't even imagine that kind of pain. In turn, I watched him pivot and turn his pain into a powerful, benevolent empire. I've witnessed the sacrifices people have made to build movements. I, myself, lost my husband and wingman, Sid. But all of us with something worth fighting for have found this soft, beautiful, loving place in our hearts to learn to continue living and contributing to others.

"I think we can all fill our hearts with that kind of love, but that requires learning, and sometimes a little time and space to understand the role hard times play in shaping us. We have to be taught or shown how to reach out to one another, to really listen to others, to share our stories. Only then can we develop empathy, which leads to generosity, and we can share that with others. Don't get me wrong, I certainly hope people don't have to experience pain. But for many, I think it can be a catalyst for becoming more generous. Maybe it's really about using experience to help clearly define one's purpose and priorities."

"Thank you for sharing, Sherrie. I'm so sorry for your loss," Emily said.

Beckstead acknowledged with a nod. No words were needed.

Emily let a little time pass, taking a long sip of tea, then continued, "I'm beginning to understand this journey I'm on, at least I think I am, but I don't have that confidence you mentioned. I still don't fully understand the process. What advice can you give about how to teach that way of thinking? Or can you even teach it?"

"That's an excellent question. Can we teach empathy or generosity? As I have grown and gained experience, I've altered my perspective on what generosity is. I believe it begins with the human spirit and with acts of grace and kindness, though for some that spirit may not come naturally."

Emily leaned in.

"I lost Sid in December 2020, and I learned a lot about generosity on another level when he was in the hospital," Beckstead continued. I realized that the medical personnel embodied *true* generosity. They couldn't leave the hospital because of Covid; my husband's surgeon didn't see his own family because if he left the hospital, he risked getting sick. He stayed to care for my family and for others' families, sacrificing time with his. That selflessness goes far beyond dedication to your profession. That is generosity! And it wasn't something the medical staff or hospital staff trained for in school."

Emily nodded, "That certainly puts the 'Heroes Work Here' signs at hospitals in a new light."

"Exactly," Beckstead said. "I share that story because it highlights innate sacrifice for the betterment of others, without any expectation of return, but it also shows how a situation was a learning experience for all of us. We leaned on one another and learned from one another. And I'd like to think younger doctors, nurses, and staff saw those acts and it was a teaching moment for them on how to truly care for patients. My point is, I do believe people can learn from and are inspired by observing others.

> **"I do believe people can learn from and
> are inspired by observing others."**

"For me, there is not a moment that I get involved in a project or assist someone that I don't think of the people who have touched my life and my family's life. And even now it sparks these memories and emotions—whether it's witnessing or participating, I've found acts of generosity touch my soul. Does that make sense?"

"It certainly does," Emily said. "Can you tell me about some of the projects you're involved in? I read about so many."

"I'm glad you asked," Beckstead said with a smile that lit up the room. "There's a newer initiative in particular I'm very excited about. I've been asked to serve on the national advisory council for the Trust for the National Mall. The Mall was getting more than thirty-five million visitors a year before the pandemic, and as a national park with that kind of usage, it needs hundreds of millions of dollars in repair and upgrades. And with so many people visiting the mall seeking educational opportunities, new experiences, and memory making, we want it to be pristine for all. As such, my work with the Mall led me to involvement with the Lockkeeper's House, which was built in 1836 and is the oldest building on the Mall, at Seventeenth Street Northwest and Constitution Avenue."

"I walked by that yesterday!" Emily excitedly jumped in. "That adorable little brick house."

Beckstead nodded with amusement. "Yes. That's the one. I've lived around Washington for a long time, and I take the Mall's nickname, 'America's front yard,' very seriously. So, I designed lock-and-key jewelry and established The Lockkeepers Collection in support of the National Mall and our history. I'm on other boards and involved in many initiatives around the District, but I'm so proud of the ability to bring awareness to the Lockkeeper's House and the Mall."

"Very cool," Emily said, thinking about how Beckstead's work touches so many people every year. "I'm sure there are a million other initiatives vying for your time and energy, so how do you choose what to work on?"

"Earlier I mentioned that I pray over decisions. But I also stick very closely to my values. I believe in doing all things with excellence, but also humility," Beckstead said. "I have to admit, though, since I lost Sid I ask questions a little differently before I say yes to things. As I said, I don't have my wingman anymore, someone who was so good at helping me lean into my strengths and reminding me of my limits. We tried to instill in our children the three T's: giving *time*, whatever *talent* one has, and, when possible, *treasure*. And now I have to make sure I'm most effectively using my time, talent, and treasure. Otherwise, I'm not serving anyone well if I'm stretched too thin to do things with the level of excellence people expect and deserve."

"Can you expand a little more on that—how you're generous with yourself?" Emily asked. "How do you guard and care for yourself? That must have been really difficult when your husband was sick."

"It was," Beckstead admitted. "We agreed that we'd care for Sid at home, so I set the alarm on the watch for every two hours, day and night, for his meds or just to check on him. My mind, my heart, and my body were all about Sid's care. Then, soon after Sid passed, I lost our fourteen-year-old dog, who had been through everything with me. And, not long after that, I had to say goodbye to our other dog. The losses kept piling up.

"One day I was standing at the kitchen sink and looked out the window, and I couldn't see what was there. I could only see these tiny blocks, like in a kaleidoscope. I thought, *Oh, darn, I'd better lie down*, and I had to hold on to the wall to get to the living room and find the couch.

It turned out I had severe nerve damage behind one eye, which I'm still working through. That's when I realized the well was running dry; I had given everything, and my body was letting me know."

"What an awful thing to go through," Emily breathed.

"This was God saying, 'Sherrie, your well is dry.' Even though self-care can sound selfish, like you're indulging yourself, that's not what it really is. If we do not take care of our mind and bodies, which are gifts and enable us to give, we have nothing. Soon after that incident, I went on a retreat and I learned to thank God for the fact that my body works, even as I woke in the morning and started my routine: Thank You for waking me, thank You for my arms and legs moving, thank You for letting me see the world around me—I became aware of the grace by which we are allowed to be who we are. That was the beginning of my healing. I don't intend to ever sacrifice my health again.

"Self-care is something we should teach at a very young age," Beckstead said. "I wish we taught young people how important it is to have five minutes in the morning to yourself and how to learn exactly who you are, which brings about confidence, and that in turn allows you to trust and form relationships. I wish we taught them that you can keep going and going only so far before you have to power down and give the hard drive a rest. During the past two years I've definitely increased my own self-care. I didn't necessarily prioritize the time before, but now I know that you have to make the time for yourself, because time doesn't wait for anybody.

> **"Self-care is something we should teach at a very young age."**

"And I'd like to clarify something," she continued.

Emily nodded.

"In the past, I took care spiritually, and I guess I got exercise by walking and going to the gym. But I didn't spend enough time on my emotional care, the kind that helps us identify who and what we are. That is why you need the quiet time. Although I know in my heart who I am, I've discovered through retreats and meditation new things about myself. For example, that I love being by myself. That quiet can be so powerful. Just sitting for thirty minutes and hearing nothing but silence clears away clutter. When we're distracted, we aren't home to receive the gifts. In that way, I learned how to take care of my emotional health on a whole new level."

"You've mentioned knowing who one is, and being confident. Do you have advice on how to grow that confidence, and I promise I'm not just asking for myself," Emily said. *Although I need all the advice I can get,* she thought.

"I understand," Beckstead said. "I mentor women in the workplace all the time, and it's an honor to do so. The first thing I would tell you is to spend time honing your list of core values, and your guiding principles. Think deeply about the person you want to become and your purpose for being here. If you know your mission and vision for yourself, confidence will come because you will know you are living by honoring what matters most to you.

"I'm happy to share some of my principles if it helps."

"Oh please!" Emily replied.

Beckstead continued. "Know who you are. Keep your promises. Learn every day. Address challenges and never avoid them. Nurture love and commitment. Do small things to make someone's day. Own your attitude. Be thankful. Begin with the end in mind. And whatever or whoever you think God is, keep God at the center of what you do."

"Perfect," Emily said. "If it's not too nosy can I ask what your mission and vision are?"

"Certainly," Beckstead replied without hesitation. "My mission and my vision remain to take bold steps forward proactively, and have a zero-tolerance policy for sexism and other prejudice. Women continue to rise in leadership and executive positions, but did you know that women of color occupy only 4 percent of C-suite positions, with white women holding another 20 percent? I see and hear of salary inequity, microaggression, bullying, nepotism, and 'othering' in the workplace all the time, and I've experienced them myself."

"So if I'm understanding you correctly, does knowing your mission, vision, and principles help you be generous because you know exactly what aligns with your purpose, which allows you to best channel your time, talent, and treasure into what matters most to you?" Emily asked. She had heard versions of this several times in other interviews, but she wanted an opportunity to try and connect the dots out loud.

Beckstead nodded in agreement but didn't directly answer the comment phrased as a question. Instead she said, "A successful woman has confidence and asks clearly for what she wants."

"That sounds exactly right," Emily said after a moment, letting the message sink in. "Going back just a little, many have said that generosity is contagious. Do you think that's true?" she asked.

"Well, contagious may not be the right word," Beckstead said with a grin. "But it certainly can be inspiring and undoubtedly spreads to others that witness the generosity. Thinking back to the example of the hospital staff who sacrificed for patients during Covid, they inspired all of us with their actions.

"That said, I tend to think generosity has to be instilled one-on-one, by parents and siblings, mentors, teachers, and friends. We learn by observing others and hearing their stories. I also believe true generosity requires a measure of self-confidence, as we spoke about, that I don't think a lot of young people have today. The pandemic had an effect here. People lost control of their choices. So I think we have to begin almost from scratch by saying, 'You have the power, you have the ability to make choices, to help, to be gracious and kind.' I want to help open their hearts and start the flow of generosity. I want it to be contagious, but in a way that doesn't come from social media. It should come from pure, internal, intentional joy."

"Yes," Emily said, "you mentioned social media and I cannot help but think it often promotes how different we are versus how similar we are. Folks I've interviewed so far make me think our world is hungry for generosity, that young people want to give of themselves and do good, but they don't know where to start."

"That's right, and there are other obstacles," Beckstead said. "In late 2022, I was involved in a small project in the District. I won't go into detail, but I will say that the experience reflected how far we all still have to go in engaging communities that don't necessary share day-to-day interaction or trusting relationships. What I loved about that project, and I learned from that project, was the reminder that trust is at the core of generosity.

"There needs to be a shift. I'm dedicated to helping with that shift toward trust. But it's going to take a lot of effort, and working with the communities."

"I admire your passion and compassion," Emily said. "Anything we can use to make the message meaningful will be important for shifting mindsets." She couldn't help but think of the challenges she might have ahead of her convincing people to trust that generosity was at the heart of being successful.

After another sip of tea, Emily asked, "Speaking of passion and compassion. Who are some of the female leaders you admire or have been role models for you?"

"Well, in the business world, I'd have to say Sheila Johnson, co-founder of Black Entertainment Television. She's also the CEO of Salamander Resorts and Hotels. Ms. Johnson's work in business, as well as philanthropy, remains the pinnacle of my admiration and inspiration. She overcame obstacles her entire life, and she lives her life with honor and grace. In the spiritual, historic world, I admire Hildegarde of Bingen, who was a Benedictine abbess of the twelfth century but was also a Renaissance woman before there was a Renaissance: she wrote poems, plays, and liturgical chants, and you can read and hear her work today. She advanced women in the church, and she was a brilliant mind in the sciences. Hildegarde spoke truth to power and was centuries ahead of her time.

"You know, sometimes I think the way to look forward is to look back. I got involved in philanthropic work early in life because people older than I was told me it was important. They were role models. Women I respected said, 'You must carry this on. You must come onto my board. You must hop on the philanthropy train right here, because you're next in charge. It will be important in your life.' These are eighty-year-old women who are still active in causes but are also recruiting. I followed the example set by the ones I trusted, who I knew were engaged in passion projects and felt the same rush from being generous as I did."

Emily could tell it was easy for women to follow Beckstead. Although she still had a million questions about the woman's remarkable life, Emily also knew she'd already heard more wisdom about becoming the woman she hoped to be than she could unpack in one sitting.

After a short, friendly battle, Beckstead insisted on paying for the tea, said her farewells, and left Peacock Alley. As Emily walked to her hotel (wishing, a bit, that she were staying at the Willard), her head buzzed with questions: *Where is my belief in God? Didn't I begin with the end in mind when I was assigned Pinafore San Diego? What am I thankful for? Which historical women do I admire?*

Mostly she wondered, *Can I be the person Don thinks I can be and wants me to be and still be authentic? Sherrie Beckstead is proof that someone, especially a woman in this world, can be many admirable things. She is the ideal model for how one can do good and, by virtue of that, also do well. That is where the magic is. That is ultimately what Don wants me to understand. But do I have what it takes to do it genuinely and graciously?*

CHAPTER 10

PEAK PERFORMANCE: MIKE KAPLAN

Emily's knuckles (and face) were white as the small passenger jet maneuvered between mountains and touched down at the Aspen-Pitkin County Airport. It was cold for early November, and the skies were layered with gray clouds, promising sleet or snow. Emily had been terrified that it would begin snowing during the short flight from Denver, making what her research had said was a "notoriously challenging airport for pilots" even more treacherous.

No snow fell, though, and the landing was steep but smooth. Emily marveled at the number of private jets lined up in a long arc on one side of the airport. *It isn't even ski season yet,* Emily thought, imagining how nice it would be to ride in a private jet.

The main building of Aspen Skiing Company (SkiCo), a rather nondescript beige building, was in the business park across from the airport. Emily was escorted to the spacious office of Mike Kaplan, who was in the process of stepping down as CEO of the company he had been responsible for shaping into a global hospitality powerhouse for the better part of twenty years. His office, too, was pretty nondescript: big U-shaped desk with windows behind it, some black leather chairs, and a blond coffee table. Photo blow-ups of skiers and mountains lined the walls. For a company of this size and scale, in a city like Aspen, it all seemed very humble. Much the way Don had described Mike.

Kaplan himself was in his late fifties, but only his graying brown hair—and the fact that he'd been with SkiCo almost thirty years—gave him away. *So many of these people don't look their age,* Emily mused. *Karma or coincidence? If I get this job with Pinafore, will I stop aging at forty?* Mike Kaplan was really pleasant-looking, with friendly eyes, a long jaw, and an unguarded smile full of white teeth. He invited Emily to sit on one of the comfy black chairs and asked her how her flight was.

"Uh, memorable," Emily said, "especially that power dive onto the runway."

"Yeah, that's intentional," Kaplan said mischievously. "We like people to know that when they get here, they're in for an adventure."

"Uh, yeah," Emily said, warming to a smile. "That's what Don told me. He also told me to tell you hi. Shall we get started? I understand you are in the process of shifting this year to sort of an emeritus position."

"Yes, kind of," Kaplan said. "I have recently supported the hiring of the two CEOs that will split my previous job, and I'm still mentoring them. I thought about stepping down for a couple years and decided that now was the best time to welcome new leadership and perspectives. After all, I'd been with the company for almost thirty years, and I became CEO in 2006. Emeritus will eventually be a good term for it."

"Tell me about Aspen Skiing Company."

"It was founded by two groups," Kaplan said. "One group was the surviving veterans of the 10th Mountain Division, which fought in the Alps during World War II. They trained in Leadville, south of Vail, not just skiing skills, but mountaineering skills. Some of them were brand-new Americans who had come from Europe before the war and wanted to fight the Nazis. They would come to Aspen for R&R. Today it's probably an hour-and-twenty-minute drive in a car, but it probably took six hours in the early 1940s, especially in winter.

"They'd come here and ski and relax, and they fell in love with the place and promised themselves they'd come back. When the war ended, a high percentage of them did return and formed the ski area. The 10th Mountain veterans came here to reset their lives and to get grounded again in humanity and nature. Anyone who goes off to war and is lucky enough to survive feels the survivor's burden to do something meaningful. These veterans made Aspen the birthplace of the modern American ski industry."

"Who was in the other group?"

"They were very different from the ski troopers: artists, industrialists, leading business thinkers, economic professors, mostly from Chicago and attached to the University of Chicago. They represented the first generation of what was called the Chicago school of economics, using economic arguments to push back against the Keynesianism that influenced the New Deal and was dominant through the 1950s. They were deep thinkers, used to reading books and discussing them among themselves, and the ones who skied came out here and discovered Aspen. The two groups met out here and recognized their common vision, to create a place that's a source of renewal for the mind, body, and spirit."

"And how did you get involved in SkiCo?" Emily asked.

"Well, my father was passionate about skiing, and my mother skied when she was pregnant with me, so I guess it's in my DNA," Kaplan replied. "I started in Taos, New Mexico, as a ski instructor in December 1986 after I graduated from the University of Colorado in Boulder. At the end of my first winter working in Taos, resort founder Ernie Blake looked at me and said, 'Kaplan, are you coming back next year?' One of the long-timers said, 'Kaplan's coming back. He's a lifer.' It hit me like a bolt of lightning—I couldn't imagine myself not skiing and instructing other people in skiing skills. I loved teaching and sharing the skiing experience. After six years in Taos, I got married and went back to school, the University of Denver, to get an MBA. That's around when I developed the aspiration to run a ski company.

"In November 1993, I was hired to be a ski school supervisor at Aspen Mountain. I remember my interview with the people who ran the ski areas and how jealous I was that they lived in Aspen. In those days, I just wanted to ski powder on steep terrain. But I knew something special was in front of me."

"What did you discover that was so special?"

"I came here to ski powder, but I stayed for the people, to turn people on to skiing and share the joy of this place and the sport with them. If you love to ski, I recommend that you get into this business and stay there. It's not easy to find a place to live. There are ups and downs. But if you stick it out, there will be opportunities. The key is to follow your passion.

"Even if you work as a ski instructor just for a season, you'll learn many of the life lessons you need to succeed anywhere else in whatever you do. You have to bring your best self every day and give that best self to the guests, to share your joy for this place. And you have to look out for each other. This is real. This is a mountain environment where the mountain can be unforgiving and unyielding, and you've got to be on. You've got to be looking after the skiers and your co-workers."

"How do you look after your skiers?" Emily asked.

"Good customer service lights the spark in everybody," Kaplan said. "It lights up the team. The people on the team realize that the more you give, the more that energy comes back to you. Part of this place, and probably the ski industry worldwide, is giving what you've learned and what you enjoy and what you love to someone else. That's really the job. Though you don't expect anything from those you are teaching, the better you do it, the more rewarding it is for you and the more successful you're going to be. It's much the same way in our hotel business.

> **"The more you give, the more that energy comes back to you."**

"The ski business isn't like a manufacturing environment, where you can control your inputs and your outputs, and you can do movement studies, efficiency studies, and productivity studies. Manufacturing is sort of cut-and-dried. It's at the command/control end of the spectrum, where the other end is the autonomous self-discovery, self-delivery model. You see that often in start-ups and among the self-employed.

"Hospitality, which includes our mountains, hotels, restaurants and other services, is probably somewhere in between. You have established standards and procedures, but you still need to have authentic interactions. On this spectrum of completely controlled to completely free, hospitality lands right in the middle. But the ski industry specifically has to have autonomy. You have a bunch of ski instructors out there teaching people skiing. You can't dictate which trail to choose for a certain skier. The terrain changes day to day, even hour to hour, and the folks in the front office don't know what the terrain is like, but the instructors do. You need to train those frontline employees in values, standards, best practices, and the processes that will lead to all the eventual successful outcomes. But after they've learned what you expect of them, they're on their own. There's a term for it among ski instructors—they call it 'guided self-discovery.' But, they know our brand and our values and they know not to compromise those things."

"How do you deal with difficult customers?"

"It takes a lot of patience. Remember how cold and snowy it got the first week of January?"

"I was in San Diego, sort of oblivious to the ski regions. Although yes, a lot of people coming from cold climates did get in a day late."

"Oof, San Diego. Can't ski there," Kaplan said. "Well, the snow was fine for skiing in Aspen, but it was awful for travel, with the airlines canceling flights right and left. By the time people reached Aspen, they were tired and cranky, because it had taken them twice as long to get here than usual. We had international customers whose flights were sixteen hours *before* delays.

"We told our team, 'Hey, people are having a hard time getting here. Let's make sure we're empathetic and give them an extra warm welcome. Don't be surprised if a lot of people are especially crabby. Just imagine how you felt the last time you were frustrated and couldn't do anything about it.' We try to see the humor in a situation and keep everything in perspective. We train our employees to handle the difficult customer, and one of our goals is to try to change that person just a tiny bit. We do that with generous acts, lots of them. Then that customer is ready to pay forward your kindness."

"Mmm, I'm imagining what hordes of inconvenienced rich people look like," Emily said.

"It wasn't pretty," Kaplan admitted. "And it's going to happen again. Don't let anyone tell you that climate change isn't happening. In our business, we see it clearly in the unpredictability of the weather, which used to be fairly consistent. Last year November was warm and dry almost till Thanksgiving. We made as much snow as we could, but it was touch and go whether we could open on time. Then the temperature plummeted, and we had lots of snow, and then of course in early

January the weather caused havoc across North America. Climate stability is important to our team and our customers. I've been to Washington to lobby for Congress to better recognize climate change issues and start to do more about it."

"That's an uphill fight," Emily said.

"You know it," Kaplan replied. "It's another reason I'm glad my team is so nimble. But it's still frustrating to see the hole we've dug, because of climate change."

"Give me another example of a situation you *could* control," Emily said.

"Okay, here's an example. One of our lifts went down for a total of forty-five minutes one day, and we gave everybody a $50 snow coupon. We probably should have given them more. Our ski patrol was at the top of the lift handing out the coupons. The idea was that the skier would finally be at the top and get a coupon and say, 'Okay, that wasn't great, but stuff happens. They acknowledged it and took care of me.' It sends that signal that the company's got your back. And the ski patrol gets that signal too, that the company goes the extra mile and lives to its values of being generous. That day could have been a public-relations disaster, but because we made things right, I came back to the office ready to go."

"I guess in a small town like Aspen, where everyone knows you and almost everyone skis, you get stopped a lot so people can tell you how to run your business."

"Well, yeah," Kaplan said. "But if people want to talk skiing, I want to hear what they have to say. It can get old, like I'm in the market and somebody asks me some deep question about snowpack or something, and I'm thinking, *I just want to pay for my milk.* But you get used to it."

"From my research, it sounds as if SkiCo pays a lot of attention to employee relations," Emily said.

"We tend to give employees a pretty long leash, because skiing is different from person to person," Kaplan said. "Instructors know how skiing feels for their own bodies, so they know their job is to help skiers discover their bodies, right down to the way the ski feels underfoot. Our instructors develop their awareness, overcome their fears, find their comfort zones. There's no one prescription on how to relate to a skier. We try to operate similarly in our other services businesses. Genuinely care about the employee and the employee will genuinely care about the customers. It's a very genuine way of working and living. Care for each other.

"Sometimes an employee makes a wrong decision, maybe with the best intentions. We aren't General Electric: we don't fire the worst-performing 10 percent every year. It's a dynamic environment and, on the practical side, it's a difficult hiring environment. Staffing is always a challenge, not just now, so it's better to coach somebody through an improvement than to cut them loose and start over with somebody new."

"Have you ever had to fire someone for incompetence?"

"I don't know, I guess so, but honestly, we try hard to find the right niche for someone or make the employee not-incompetent. We had an employee, Tom, selling lift tickets who really wasn't suited to work face-to-face with the public. The perception was he wasn't very nice to people, to the point that we would get complaints about him. Part of it was just his face. He looked like he was frowning, even when he wasn't. People want the folks who sell them stuff to be perky and friendly, and this guy just wasn't. Another company might have let him go, but we realized he just needed to work a little bit less directly with customers, so we made him a supervisor, who worked more behind the scenes and not at the counter. He stuck with us for thirty years after that. The funny thing was that toward the end, he was kind of a mentor for the youngest employees. They knew he genuinely cared and they kind of liked his crabbiness, and he knew how to resolve any problem the customer had.

"One year the community went through a contentious discussion about the airport. It basically boiled down to a growth/no growth argument. Some people wanted the airport to grow to allow more and bigger aircrafts. Others wanted it to stay the size it was so as not to encourage big planes. And some who lived under the flight path even wanted the airport to be shut down altogether and moved to a more rural area. I was on the 'vision' committee, and everybody figured that as the man from SkiCo, I'd want unfettered growth and more airplanes, but that's not where I was at all. We wanted a balanced approach.

Therefore, engaging in a process involving so many longtime locals meant that everyone in the room had a lot of history with the company and with me personally as its leader. That's because as the ski area operator in this small valley, it's nearly impossible to separate company from community. Just about everyone has a relative or housemate working at the company and has a stake in the company's decisions and actions. So what happens at work never stays at work. Internal emails sent to all employees are shared with the local papers. And the inevitable workplace dramas or disagreements often become talk at the dinner table, on the chairlift, in the grocery store, and even amongst local elected officials.

This committee was comprised of local residents living under the flight path, former mayors, former employees, heads of HOA's, and of course skiers, environmentalists, and business leaders. Nearly everyone in that room must have had some story to tell about when the company got sideways with them or made a decision they disagreed with. Despite all that baggage, virtually everyone ended up being a very positive contributor to the process, very balanced, and very supportive of my views and perspective. One example, after the fact, I found out that one of those participants had been married to Tom for many years. She was grateful to us for treating him right and giving him a job that showed we understood and cared for him. There's some positive karma for you. Who would have thought?"

"That's really powerful."

"A big part of good employee relations just involves sincerely caring, looking people in the eye and acknowledging them as individuals. On New Year's Day, I walk around the slopes and the hotels and say 'Thank you for working' to everyone who's on the job. They appreciate that. Even when it isn't New Year's Day, it's important to look at employees as more than just cogs in a machine. Have a conversation, engage them in some positive way. The idea is to acknowledge that we're both human beings sharing the same space. Once it becomes a practice, you start to think, *How can I do more of this? How can I acknowledge people in a broader, more generous, more systemic way?* When you get to that point, you start to think, *When we see a problem in the community, can we help solve that problem?*"

> "Once it becomes a practice, you start to think, *How can I do more of this?*"

"How did you operate during the Covid-19 pandemic?"

"Boy, that was something," Kaplan replied. "We had to reinvent the entire playbook without clear rules and operate in a way that ensured the safety of the community. The gondolas were a big problem, with people sharing enclosed cabins. And of course, we couldn't run the restaurants and a lot of the hotel resort features the way we usually did.

"We had to furlough dozens of people for the duration, which felt terrible. We said, 'Oh my gosh! All these people are suddenly out of work. What are they going to do?' We had to feed them, so we brought all the food in the refrigerators down from the mountains and gave it away. Then we set up a mobile, Covid-safe food pantry in the valley. It ran for a full year. Our events people did that, because obviously we weren't having events for a while. We got great publicity from it, so it was a little self-serving, but we sincerely cared for these people, we knew we wanted them to stay in the community, and nobody knew how long the pandemic was going to last.

"After we closed for Covid, we also made grooming the mountains a way for people to ski for free. A lot of people like to hike up and ski down, and that's best done on groomed snow. It's almost like mowing the lawn; grooming smooths out the snow and makes it magical. But if it's ungroomed, especially after a couple of days, it gets pretty gnarly. Our teams just said, 'Hey, we've got these employees who are all stuck here. We should groom the mountain so they can ski and have a good time.' It was an easy thing for me to approve, even though it cost a bunch of money; it was the right thing to do. So we groomed the mountains as long as there was snow. There was always at least one path down each of the four mountains. You wouldn't believe how many thank-yous I got, how much love I got for that, even though it wasn't my idea."

"I can imagine," Emily said. "You really care about your employees. How else do you take care of them?"

"We want to encourage and make it okay for the employees to experience the product, to be the customer. I think it's a collective obligation, theirs and ours. Most of the hospitality business misses that completely. To be a good server, it really helps to have been served. Just like to be a good customer, it's helpful if you've been on the service end. It makes you more knowledgeable about the product and more empathetic with your co-workers. It also sparks creative ideas: An employee experiencing the product might come up with something we never thought about before.

"So we have an employee-stay program where every employee stays at each of our hotels for two to four nights for free, space permitting. It really renews the spirits of our workers, because they get to eat the meals in our restaurants and stay in our rooms and ski the powder on our mountains. Employee stays encourage employees to say to themselves, *I get to be pampered in the hotel, then I get to pamper other people. I've got more to give our customers because my tank's been filled by my employers, and I've also seen my work from the customer's side.* It's just who we are. I hope we never lose that perspective and understanding of how things come back full circle."

"That's amazing," Emily said. "I've never heard of a company doing that before. You do a lot for your employees, come to think of it. I read that SkiCo spent $12 million to raise everyone's pay by three dollars an hour, and you're investing another $18 million in employee housing and a childcare facility."

"Yes, some see that as being generous, but we see it as just being practical," Kaplan said. "For the employees to be able to really show up to work every day, they've got to have a good home life and they've got to have security. That's harder than ever. This is a community of millionaires and billionaires, and most of our staff can't afford to live anywhere near Aspen. Affordable rentals are an hour or more away. I won't pretend to say we're there, but we're trying.

"Don't forget, there's an upside for us. It's like this past spring, after the season, when we shut down the entire operation for two weeks, even the front office, and everybody got two weeks off with pay. That was a cost-cutting move, because for two weeks we didn't have overhead costs, we didn't have to buy food for the restaurants, and so forth."

"Still, that's a very nice thing to do for your staff."

"I really believe in servant leadership," Kaplan said. "That's the business philosophy in which the goal of the leader is to serve—serve both customers and employees. In traditional leadership, the leader's focus is for the company or NGO to thrive, to take in as much money as possible and keep profits or donations as high as possible. Not here. We all do what needs to be done, and the bottom line is secondary to providing a wonderful experience for our customers. In the end, our bottom line does just fine.

"I really believe in servant leadership."

"I've washed dishes with those guys. I've changed sheets with the housekeepers. And not just me, the whole executive team. We have a text system where if anyone needs help somewhere, it goes out to the whole team and we swarm it. We show up and we just do the job till it's done, whatever it takes. I think the working-side-by-side, servant-leadership approach is pretty powerful. It demonstrates what we believe at our core.

"I'm not saying there isn't a financial angle for the company. The idea of executives working alongside employees came out after the economy went sideways in 2008. We were thinking about expense management. But the program is really important to this day. Management gets to see how their decisions play out. I spent last Christmas Day loading one of the lifts, and I can't think of a better way to spend the day.

"I think this community and this company have a very strong culture, one that I would call values-based, where skiing and hospitality are important but community is also important. We live those values and take stands on them," Kaplan said. "How you treat people, how you communicate, how you make decisions. There are always tradeoffs, but I'd like to think our values are apparent in our decisions."

"Besides skiing, how else do you keep your tank filled?" Emily asked.

"For me, it starts and ends with the people," Kaplan said. "You spend so much time at work and immersed in this place, and at the end of the day, it's who you're spending time with and how you all behave when things get tough—and how you celebrate when things go well. I have an incredible team: inspiring, rewarding, amazing. I'm honored that they listen to me once in a while.

"Here's a good example. One day my tank was empty. I was in the office just grinding through my emails and coming off the busy holiday period. I just wasn't feeling it. I was forcing myself to do my work. Finally, it was 1:30 and I hadn't had lunch, so I thought I'd better eat. But instead of going somewhere I could walk to, I decided to go up one of the mountains and get lunch at the top. I went to Two Creeks, which is a short drive from here. Sure enough, the second I got out of my car I bumped into a friend whose wife taught my kids. We just had a short conversation, but it picked me up a little bit. Then I decided to go up the hill to take one run before lunch, and when I got on the lift, there were three SkiCo instructors in the chair. All first-year, all amazing people. We had a great conversation, and I came back to the office rejuvenated."

"Your tank got replenished," Emily said.

"That's right. Sharing my time, connecting with people, and taking that run down the mountain did it for me. Sometimes I feel guilty because that kind of thing takes time away from work, but then I realize, *No, Mike, you aren't playing hooky. You're refilling your tank so you can work with enthusiasm and you're doing your job by taking a run with team members and customers and having lunch at one of our restaurants.*

"It feels like cheating, because the sun's out and it's a beautiful day, and the snow is amazing. It's a little unfair, because we're not making widgets. We're skiing and hosting people in our beautiful hotels. The product is so wonderful that I think it makes the routine work a little easier. If you can't tell, I love everything about skiing and sharing it with others. It is good for my heart."

"You sound as if you wish everybody could live this life."

"I do. I mean not everybody loves snow and altitude and skiing, but I wish everyone who wanted to work at a resort could get a chance to do it—here, Hawaii, Italy, Aruba, anywhere. I'm so grateful that I've been able to do this work for my entire career. That guy in Taos was right: I'm a lifer.

"This place was always meant to be more than just a ski resort," Kaplan said. "What we try to do is share the joy because, one, it feels like the right thing to do. It's so wonderful to live here and get up here every day and experience the things that we do that it feels selfish; it feels like you've just got to share. What you come to learn is that the more you share, the more rewarding it is. You see the lights go on in the customer's eyes, and you build a connection with them. To live vicariously through them is so rewarding. It took me a while, but as I matured, I started to realize that sharing what we have and experiencing it through the eyes of the customer is almost more fun than experiencing it myself.

"A lot of times you've sort of got your head down and you aren't looking at the beauty of it all, so it's important to look up and see what you have. Beauty exists everywhere, in every job, and in every place. For sure if you live in, let's say, Detroit, and you work at a manufacturing plant, you have to look harder for the beauty than you do here. But the beauty, and the fulfillment, are there, and if you take that little extra time to discover them and share them, I think the sharing becomes contagious."

"You aren't the first executive to tell me that generosity is contagious," Emily said.

"It absolutely is," Kaplan said. "Sharing is contagious. Happiness is contagious. I think generosity in general is contagious. You're always going to have your percentage of people who seem to be out for themselves. Cultures can encourage that too. If the culture is more about self at the expense of others, that's contagious, too, right? Certain businesses might tend to be more like that: Wall Street and some forms of real estate come to mind. But if you create a culture of generosity when you're leading, the generosity becomes contagious. It may be easier here, but it can be done anywhere in any business with the right focus and the right leadership.

> "If you create a culture of generosity when you're leading, the generosity becomes contagious."

"I think by nature most people want to be generous. We're wired that way. Humans are social animals, and I think being connected to others and getting positive reinforcement triggers a positive response in our brains. It's something we want more of. I think for the most part generosity can be trained and then reinforced. It can be something that's just the norm, and people will fall into that, at least relative to the way other businesses are run. It's easier in a small community like this, but I believe more and more that the whole world is a small community. Technology has brought us together in so many ways, and what goes around comes around whether a community is big, medium, or small. There's always an upside to generosity, and no one has shown me a downside yet."

"Thank you," Emily said. "I think that does it. You've been a terrific interview subject."

"Great!" Kaplan said. "Where are you staying tonight?"

"Your company was kind enough to put me up at the Little Nell," Emily said.

"Oh, you'll love it. All the rooms are beautiful. It's right near the gondola, so go up and see the view if you have time tomorrow. And it's on the edge of the village, so you can walk around and imagine what Aspen looked like before Fendi and Prada invaded."

Emily smiled and looked out one of the big office windows. The snow she had dreaded all day was starting to fall from the lead-colored sky. Somehow, it didn't seem so threatening now.

"Oh, look, it's starting to snow," she said.

Kaplan looked out the window, and a big smile spread across his face.

"Yesss!" he exclaimed, pumping his fist. "I've been waiting for this since April. We don't open for a couple of weeks, but if this keeps up, I may have something to ski on tomorrow. Don't worry, you'll get out okay," he assured Emily, whose brow had furrowed. "The pilots who fly in and out of here can make it through nearly anything."

"I'm glad to hear it," Emily said. *Wait . . . nearly anything?* she thought.

"Aw, this is great," Kaplan said, turning to Emily and beaming. "This is the *real* Aspen!"

CHAPTER 11

CULTURAL CURRENCY: AYMAN EL-MOHANDES

Emily hadn't been in New York since she graduated from Cornell, and she felt almost assaulted by the rush and noise when she entered the city. She'd clearly become a West Coast girl in the last few years. She got out of the subway with what felt like hundreds of other people and headed up to street level to look around.

The main office tower for City University of New York's graduate programs was on 125th Street between Fifth Avenue and Lenox, and Emily strolled over to the building taking in the sights and sounds. The street has a long history of art and culture. If she recalled correctly, it was *the* corridor of the African American renaissance in the US. The Apollo Theater and the "A" train that inspired Duke Ellington's piano piece were right here.

After a short walk from Lenox to the front doors of the building, Emily took an elevator to the seventh floor. She expected the office of Ayman El-Mohandes to be just another professor's glorified walk-in closet, but Dr. El-Mohandes's was spacious; furnished with club chairs, a sofa, and a large, ornately carved wooden desk; and filled with so many art works of African and Asian origin that Emily thought she had stumbled into the office of an anthropology professor. Dr. El-Mohandes himself, who rose when Emily walked in, was the model of a college administrator: gray-haired, gray-bearded, and bespectacled, in a spotless dark suit and tie.

Emily knew that, in a long career, El-Mohandes had gone to medical school in his native Cairo and been a successful pediatrician and neonatologist for many years before switching to public health. He was among the founding faculty of a school at GW, opened a public-health graduate school in Nebraska, then jump-started the program at CUNY, doubling its applicants and doing five times the research.

El-Mohandes extended his hand in greeting. "Welcome, Emily," he said.

"I would have mistaken your office for an art gallery," Emily said, wide-eyed.

"Each piece has a special memory for me," the professor said. "Although I am a scientist and an academic, I grew up in a family where half the family members were scientists and mathematicians, but the other half were artists and art-inclined, so I have that interest in my blood. Most of the objects are steeped in the native art tradition where people in Africa and Asia and New Guinea applied their talents to natural materials."

Sensing Emily's interest in his story, he continued.

"I have a large collection of African art in ceramics and metal," he added, "weaves from Asia, and bark art that my wife brought back from Papua New Guinea. Perhaps I was an anthropologist in another life, because I value these objects not only for their aesthetic value but for how they represent their peoples' culture and humanity."

El-Mohandes ushered Emily to one of the club chairs. She took a seat and continued to admire her surroundings.

"As you know," she began, "Don has tasked me with traveling around the United States to interview a number of people on the role generosity plays in their lives and the lives of others. And I really think I'm starting to get it. But I'd love to start by hearing more about your upbringing; did generosity play a large role in how you were raised?"

"First, I have great respect for Don. I hope to see him again soon. You have a great mentor there. Regarding my youth, I grew up in a family of physicians," the professor said. "Both my parents were physicians, and my mother was a pioneer in Egypt. She graduated from medical school in 1941 and became one of the first pediatric neurologists in the Middle East. So I grew up with parents who had really dedicated their lives to service.

"There is such a thing as being generous to excess, and I saw both of my parents contribute their time, energy, and even health beyond what is considered excessive. They contributed of themselves in very direct ways that I don't think I will be able to replicate. But their generosity inspired me. And I witnessed the joy it brought."

"That does sound like an issue with balance. I want to hear more about that later. Did you have other doctors in your extended family?" Emily asked.

"Yes, but one of the people who was also an influence on me was my mother's oldest sister, my aunt, who probably was among the first formally trained social workers in Egypt; she graduated from the Institute of Social Work in the early thirties and she died in her mideighties. She had always been extremely giving, having been sent to French Catholic schools in Alexandria. We called her the Egyptian Muslim Nun. She dedicated her life to service, and when she died, there were dozens of people out on the street mourning her, people that we didn't know, whom we had never met, but whose lives she had affected.

"I remember very, very well an adult man who had had poliomyelitis and walked with a pronounced limp. He was from an impoverished family in a small cotton-mill town, and said that without my aunt, he would have been neglected in a bedroom of his parents' home because he was crippled. My aunt literally extracted him from darkness and explained to his mother that because he was challenged in that way, he needed extra help, not less, and he needed more opportunity, not less. Because of my aunt, he completed his education, became an accountant, and lived a normal life. My mother's sister had affected his destiny in a way that could be done only by people who contributed of themselves directly to others."

"She was not only generous with her efforts but also forward-thinking," Emily said.

"Indeed, she was," El-Mohandes said. "My family was always very generous to me, and my wife is a generous person, so it came to me naturally, and I have always had role models for it. Generosity became a legacy of how we live. It doesn't necessarily have a religious platform in my life, but it has a spiritual platform and a social platform. I have been lucky enough through the years to nurture generosity in myself in part by examples of many people around me who have inspired me.

"Let me tell you a story. Eight years after graduating from medical school, I came to the United States and worked as a pediatrician and neonatologist in Washington, DC's Children's Hospital. I was shocked to see the social and health mayhem created by the crack-cocaine epidemic in Washington in the mideighties and felt a sense of desperation that no one was addressing the root cause of what we were seeing in the intensive care unit: the birth of extremely premature babies by very young mothers who had fallen victim to this epidemic.

"Many of these babies died because neonatal medicine was not that advanced at the time, and many of them lived with long-term needs. It occurred to me one very hot night that we were not really addressing the problem, and I felt as if my long training as a physician had not prepared me to deal with the drug crisis that spurred the premature births—so I decided I needed to enter the world of public health."

"How old were you at that time?"

"Somewhere in my thirties. At the time, I had two children at home and was working in an ICU, plus pursuing research to become tenured in the School of Medicine. But I began work on a degree in public health, driven by a sense of duty. When I look back on it, I must have been crazy, because my life was very busy, and again, my wife and I had two children, and she traveled a great deal for her work in banking. But she was dedicated to being supportive of me and our children, and I dedicated time and energy to learn new skills and do my share of the childcare.

"That teamwork allowed me to earn my degree in public health. It took me four years to finish that master's degree because I had to take it a bit at a time, but when I graduated, it transformed my life, not to mention my understanding of life, health, and priorities. The personal satisfaction my wife and I took in our sacrifices meant our generosity was well rewarded."

Emily nodded.

"The phrase 'social determinants of health' hadn't been coined when I went into public health," El-Mohandes continued. "But in the very early nineties, I started to read about them. One study, which I found quite weird, claimed that you could prevent babies from being born prematurely by just sending somebody to the homes of women who had very limited resources. That person would fluff up the pregnant woman's pillows, put some food in the refrigerator, maybe vacuum the carpet, and leave.

"My medical training caused me to be extremely skeptical of this; I mean, how unscientific! What do you do for a pregnant woman by fluffing her pillows and vacuuming her carpet? And that led me to design my first study that looked at self-efficacy."

"What did you propose?" Emily asked, truly curious.

"When I wrote the grant proposal, titled 'Pride in Parenting,' I expanded on what the earlier study had done, but I didn't think it was going to work. We recruited women who had just given birth and had received no prenatal care during pregnancy, and we sent them trained, nonjudgmental home visitors. Along with helping these women with chores and problem solving, we organized groups of new mothers who helped each other. We didn't give them money to go to the doctor or vouchers for taxis; we just helped them identify resources that were available and helped them organize their lives.

"And we found that with this help, these women with limited resources would develop a can-do attitude and improve their lives if given the opportunity to reach within themselves and find strength."

"That's amazing," Emily said.

She began to wonder about some of the lives the various staff at Pinafore San Diego lived away from their jobs. She had at times been impatient with their excuses for being late and their claims of being tired. His example gave some potential context, providing her with more understanding of, and empathy for, their situations. She winced at her lack of compassion.

"You have to allow yourself space and time," El-Mohandes was saying, "and you have to allow it to everybody else. Taking the time to learn more about another can help us all have a little more grace. I can be endlessly patient at certain times. But my family will tell you that when it comes to practical matters, sometimes I am not able to listen enough, or I want to get to the end point quickly.

"Taking the time to learn more about another can help us all have a little more grace."

"Sometimes my impatience with routine life happens because I feel mundane affairs matter less, that there are bigger cosmic conditions that matter more. Those conditions need our collective energy to move things forward, and they require more than your daily physical commitment. On the other hand, I observe things that are happening in front of me.

"It helps that I'm basically an optimist. Ever since I was a child, I've had this feeling that I belong to something good, something that's moving in the right direction, and that I have a part in. I have a high level of trust, which is in its way a blessing, because I can be positive under dire circumstances. I define generosity as a quality by which you can afford not to be reactive to people who mistreat or are suspicious or are sometimes unnecessarily accusatory or limiting. There's a lot of space before you need to protect your own integrity. I think being tolerant of others is a form of generosity. It is an attitude toward the balance of good, so long as you determine how much energy you're going to put toward the good.

"I think people oftentimes mistake going above and beyond the boundaries of where most people's energy ends as generosity. But in fact, if you exceed your limits, that isn't necessarily generous because you end up not taking care of yourself mentally, emotionally, or physically. When, in fact, small actions and kind choices can enable others to be generous, and I've found that even small gestures come back to you in significant ways."

Emily nodded and leaned forward.

**"I've found that even small gestures come
back to you in significant ways."**

"You were asked to establish a public health school in Nebraska," she said, thinking back to the guidance Don had provided her, "which is growing but still smaller than other medical schools and universities. Was it easier there to develop the energy you speak of than in New York?"

"New York didn't intimidate me. Remember, I was born and raised in Cairo, one of the largest and busiest cities in the world," El-Mohandes said. "I was accustomed to navigating amid crowds and finding clarity of direction and safety of pathway within hordes of people. Washington, DC, felt like a small town compared to Cairo.

"The entire state of Nebraska has one-fourth the population of New York City, which itself is much less populous than Cairo. So coming to New York was like a homecoming to me. It was freeing rather than limiting or challenging, and it was enabling rather than disabling.

"It was in Nebraska, where I lived for four years as the first permanent dean of a new school of public health, that I found a challenging environment. I had never lived in an environment in the United States that was at odds with my background, thinking, and, at times, beliefs. Further, my wife, Hala, remained in Washington with the children and had a full-time position in export finance. We had a long-distance marriage for those four years while I was in a foreign setting navigating uncharted waters."

"My goodness!" Emily exclaimed. That barely worked with friends, let alone a romantic relationship, she knew.

El-Mohandes nodded and smiled.

"My job, of course," he explained, "was to examine the public health environment in Nebraska. It's a relatively healthy state, but with pockets of discrimination and isolation, and Nebraska has a century-long history of importing Mexican laborers to help with the corn industry. I feel Nebraska should be grateful to the Mexican people who leave their communities and help the agricultural economy, but unfortunately the governor of Nebraska at the time decided to block measures that would cover prenatal care for undocumented Mexican immigrants.

"It didn't make sense economically, because one disastrous pregnancy could cost the state half a million dollars. A group of policy advocates including me were able to convince the Nebraska legislature to vote for legislation that would protect undocumented women, and when the governor vetoed the bill, I was able to get enough votes to overturn the veto, an unheard-of occurrence. But I knew it was my responsibility to advocate for those women and children.

"I'm proud of that accomplishment, but I did so against the grain of the political culture, and I felt I could do more, so when New York called, I felt it was more aligned with my philosophy and was the place I should be."

"I like that word *advocate*. How does that translate into your role as an educator? How do you impart generosity to students?" Emily asked.

"I think students are more likely to be generous when they feel appreciated, and because they're appreciated, they're able to give more and take more. Young people need to feel that they are trusted and be able to work with dignity. Our students at CUNY are New Yorkers, working, parenting, learning, commuting, and with all their responsibilities we find that circumstances outside their control often dictate their challenges. We always want our students to know how much we appreciate them and trust them.

"For example, during the Covid pandemic, it was a challenge for many of our students to pay their tuition, but the university had a policy that students couldn't get their degrees unless the tuition was paid. I was uncomfortable with that, so we took it on ourselves to raise money through philanthropic efforts to give grants to students that allowed them to pay their debts and graduate.

> "I think being tolerant of others
> is a form of generosity."

"I had one student who had paid her tuition throughout her coursework, but she had hit a financial roadblock during her last semester, spring 2020. She'd been floating from one sublet to another, whatever she could afford, and had been living with a roommate, a woman she didn't really know, since the fall. Her roommate became one of the first Covid casualties in New York, and my student not only was stuck with her half of the rent but she paid for the woman's burial, because the roommate apparently had no close family who could claim her. She couldn't pay her tuition, so we offered her a grant. And imagine—she said no. 'I don't need this money, somebody else needs it more,' she said. 'I will work and I will pay my tuition.'"

"Wow," Emily said, nodding in awe.

"I told my students that if I were subjected to the pressures that they have survived, I would not have gone on. I would have shriveled into a dry little prune in the corner of a room and died. What generosity did I show compared to the generosity of this young woman who was ready to interrupt her future, her career, her prospects, her dreams to give every dollar she had for the burial of someone she barely knew? And when offered the money to pay her bills said no, somebody else deserves it more than me? Maybe we were generous with our time to raise this money for the students, but compared to this woman, I'm an embarrassment."

"She seems pretty well suited to a public health career that basically is about taking care of others," Emily mused.

"It is a continuum," El-Mohandes agreed. "She had to have been raised by strong and generous people. You can teach children about generosity only by example, because if they are in that circle of generosity, then they are witness to its incredible magical results that cannot be told, that have to be experienced and observed. And they have to understand that the rewards, tangible and intangible, are observable. It is not only the tangible things that are observable. The intangible things—love, gratitude, compassion, companionship, community, support, identity, strength—are all observable. They're not easily quantifiable or measurable, but they are very observable. I am proud of how generous both my daughters are, actually, and again it comes to them naturally.

"When you raise your children in an environment in which generosity is a natural commodity that is shared, then they expect to see that reward, which in turn energizes their bend toward generosity. They expect it, they want it, they thrive in it, and without it, they feel their lives are incomplete and empty.

"The children I feel sorry for are the ones who aren't brought up to be generous, because they don't get the positive feedback. They don't miss it, but their lives are less fulfilling without it. In the Egyptian dialect of Arabic, we have an expression where we say a person is 'missing a part.' The person is okay, even likable, but he is not complete spiritually."

"Can you overcome that?" Emily asked. "When I was in college, we all talked about wanting to be good people, but that was mostly, 'Someday I'll have the means and capacity to make the world better.' A lot of us didn't grow up in households where generosity was important. But I also have examples where the trait was innate to the person himself or herself and not intergenerationally acquired."

"It isn't easy," El-Mohandes said. "And a lot of it is cultural. I grew up at a time and in a segment of Egyptian society where you mostly didn't need anything. Either your parents met your needs, or you had a lot of your needs met by government, through different forms of public systems.

"In that environment, although my parents were not poor by any standard, we lived in a community where a very large segment of the population was needy, but the safety net wasn't created by the government, with programs like Social Security and Medicaid. The safety net was created by social contract, basically people taking care of those who had less.

"Historically in Egypt, it was expected that the big landowner would contribute toward the well-being of those less fortunate than themselves in the rural environment, and although that was generally a form of charity, in many cases it was an unspoken contract that even within one family, those who *had* would help those who did *not* have.

"I hope our students, whether they grew up in a generous environment or not, come to think of generosity in its truest sense as a commodity. Call it a social commodity, call it a spiritual commodity, call it an economic commodity, call it a philosophical or political commodity, but at the end of the day we all give and take. And being generous with others, while respecting our own boundaries, can have an exponential impact on people and communities.

"You see, there is this multiplier factor to generosity where suddenly it is like an investment. You start small, and then something happens, this magic yeast that is put into this dough, and then it grows and it grows and it grows.

> "There is this multiplier factor to generosity. You start small, and then it grows and it grows and it grows."

"You can treat giving your time and love like one would money, as if it's an investment fund, a start-up, but well-thought-out. You recruit people that have the intention, but perhaps didn't experience the environment, to allow them to invest in this fund. They say, 'Oh, wow, I've been looking for a fund like this, yes, I'm with you,' and they jump in.

"The fund gets bigger and bigger, the payouts more and more meaningful. People who invested with you realize, 'I know what to do now,' and they start their own funds, and those funds get bigger. All because someone said, 'I have this little investment fund; would you like to invest with me?'"

"Is it really that simple?" Emily asked skeptically.

"It is, quite often. Just look at our students who go back out into the boroughs, into communities and homes, and dedicate their lives to sharing and practicing their knowledge about how to be healthier, happier, safer, live longer. Once they leave our program each individual oes on to touch so many lives," El-Mohandes said, nodding.

"That sounds amazing, and like a tremendous amount of...paperwork," Emily chuckled. "Let me ask you something different," she said, absorbing the point about a ripple effect. "Given all your responsibilities, how are you generous with yourself, physically and mentally? How do you fill your own tank? You stated earlier that your parents weren't good at this. Are you?"

"Well, for one thing, I surround myself with beauty," El-Mohandes said, looking around his office. "It is a source of light for me. And I'm very aware of the aesthetic energy around me. I appreciate things, I take photographs of them, I listen to music, and I read. I'm also protective of my alone time, possibly because I grew up an only child, with a lot of solitude. I find alone time to be absolutely essential to define the territory around me and redefine myself. Moments of silence and quiet are very effective in rejuvenating my energy.

"But I also like to congregate with small groups of people who are of similar energy to mine. There is a spiritual path called the Sufi Path, and when you travel along it, you will encounter the Sufi Circle. In a Sufi Circle, people meditate together in a circle, and the belief is that they invigorate each other's energy. There's a multiplier effect on the energy, and if one person in the circle is sad, or skeptical, or just not attuned to the rest of us, we will say 'Oh, somebody is heavy today,' and we will use our energy to try to elevate that person. I find it to be valuable social reinforcement to be with people who are similarly inspired."

"Do you feel that your generosity has been rewarded during your lifetime?" Emily asked.

"More than rewarded," El-Mohandes said modestly. "I am very realistic about who I am and what I am, and I don't see myself close to being halfway or even a quarter of the way toward perfection. Happily, I am not trying to reach perfection. What I ask for in exchange for whatever work I have done for society is that some kind of good comes from my work, that a community or society at large experiences growth, comfort, and security.

"The thanks and honors and accolades are lovely, but seeing results from my work, and admiring my family and their generous spirit, is the currency that rewards me. And seeing students go out and carry on the work is rewarding."

Emily put aside her notebook.

"I think we can stop there, Dr. El-Mohandes," she said, deeply impressed with the doctor's modesty and firmness of beliefs. "Thank you very much, and thank you for this look at the beautiful and striking objects in your office."

"It is my pleasure," El-Mohandes said. "You have given me a moment of contemplation and have allowed me to relive emotions that are purifying, and you have also given me solace and comfort."

Emily was taken aback. "I have?"

"Yes," the professor said. "This has been a pleasant interlude. Your time and attention is a generous gift you have given me."

Emily left the building on 125th Street and entered a cacophony of honking, sirens, and loud conversations. *Hello, New York,* she thought. *It was so nice in Dr. El-Mohandes's office.* Today was a beautiful day—not terribly hot or humid, and almost cloudless—so Emily headed down Fifth Avenue. She had a compelling desire to take in the borough's unique art and houses where the likes of James Baldwin and Langston Hughes once created their work.

CHAPTER 12

EMBRACING OKAY-NESS: ANDY HILL

The weather back in Denver was just like Emily had expected it to be: dry, crisp, clean. The best of mile-high air. She loved how nature stretched over the buildings in this part of Colorado, the mountains commanding and tall in the background as the sky extended forever. *Andy really chose a great home base for his office.* Straightening her skirt, she headed up the walkway to meet Andy Hill.

Just inside the door, Emily startled, then grinned. The first thing that greeted her as she walked through the frosted glass doors was a moose head mounted on the wall. *Don didn't tell me he hunts,* Emily thought. Then she noticed that while the moose had realistic antlers, its face had a cartoonish appearance, with wide, surprised eyes. When did Dr. Seuss work in 3D? It was certainly the right style.

"I see you've met Morris," Andy Hill said from behind his big desk. He rose and approached Emily, hand outstretched.

"Um, yes," she said, shaking Hill's hand. She pointed her thumb back toward the moose head. "Am I mistaken, or is Morris there a creation of Dr. Seuss?"

"You are not mistaken," Hill said. "Before he wrote children's books, Ted Geisel made seventeen wall-mounted pieces of animals, birds, and fish. He used real animal parts, mostly bones and bony structures like beaks and antlers, but they aren't real taxidermy, and he gave all the creatures Seussian faces. This is a copy."

"That is *awesome*," said Emily, who had grown up on Dr. Seuss books.

> "Generosity may not come back exactly when you expect it to or how you expect it to, but it will always come back in some way."

Hill pointed behind his desk to a full-sized framed oil painting of a large, happy-looking dog, tongue hanging out. "And that's Ozzie."

"I want to give him a big hug," Emily said.

"He's been with me in a lot of different offices," Hill said, looking contentedly at the portrait of his beloved companion. "He puts a smile on my face, and usually on other people's faces too. I love artwork that communicates emotion and message, and I want visitors to know that things aren't too serious here."

"Well, Morris and Ozzie certainly do that."

"Let's sit over here," Hill said, indicating a cozy corner with two overstuffed chairs and a small coffee table. Emily sat down, feeling as if she had known Andy Hill her entire life, like he'd been her babysitter or something. He exuded reliability, confidence, and good humor.

"Don told me all about your project, so you don't have to explain it to me," he said, leaning forward expectantly. "Would you like a coffee or glass of water?"

"I'm great, no thank you," Emily said.

"Where would you like to begin?" he asked.

"With your early life," Emily replied. "Childhood, education, all of it. I'm all ears!"

"Sure," Hill said, settling into his chair. "I grew up in a loving family, I think. My dad was in the military until I was about eight, then we settled in San Antonio. When I was about fourteen, my three older siblings all moved out within about a six- to nine-month period, and my parents decided it was time to wonder if they wanted to stay together.

"Then my mom disappeared and was gone for quite a while. My parents weren't really connected at the time. I felt like my siblings had better parenting than I did. I used to go to church alone, because I was expected to go, with kind of a chip on my shoulder; my siblings got the nice family experience, and look what I got.

"We were Mormons, which means our lifestyle and culture, the friends we could have, even our roles within the family were clearly delineated. There were boundaries you weren't supposed to cross. And I stayed with it long enough to go on my mission for the LDS Church for two years. *That* was an experience. You're told what time to wake up and what to do every single hour. You can't listen to popular music or read magazines, and during my mission, you could only speak to your family twice a year.

"When you go on a mission for the LDS Church for the first time, you're assigned to be with another person for twenty-four hours a day. The first guy I was assigned had a dad who was in prison because he had almost killed someone; it was all over the news. That put my own family in perspective.

"I remember thinking I had it good. I have had things happen, difficulties in my family, but geez, I have it better than so many people. That mission was tough, but I left it with a sense of gratitude for what the universe had dealt me, and even though I wound up leaving the church, I think there were a lot of positive things that I drew from my experiences growing up."

"When did you leave the church?" Emily asked, intrigued by his upbringing, so radically different from her own.

"I guess in my midthirties," Hill replied, thinking back. "By that time I'd married a woman and had three kids. I had checked all the boxes and done everything that I was supposed to do, but I still found something missing. I had to examine whether my religion fit within my belief system, and I discovered that it did not. That's a tough place to be for a Mormon. Leaving my religion meant potentially leaving my family, all my friends, and anyone I had a close relationship with. Often if you leave the LDS Church, your family won't talk to you again. So I started therapy and really learned a lot about myself."

Emily nodded and waited for more. Hill paused and reflected.

"The main thing I gained from that period," he continued, "was that my okay-ness was assured. No matter what happened to me, no matter what went on in my life, I was going to be okay. And understanding that, knowing that no event, no person, nothing could threaten my okay-ness, really gave me the strength to let my family know I was leaving. After that, I let go of a mental barrier to my sexuality as well and allowed myself to go to a place where I could think about the possibility that I was gay. That was never a door for me to open, so what would happen if I opened it?"

"It sounds almost as if leaving the church was harder than coming out," Emily said, fascinated.

"Not harder, but all pieced together," Hill said. "I was a happy person before I began to consider both leaving the church and coming out, but I wasn't being my authentic self, which doesn't necessarily have to do with sexuality. I found in therapy and through a lot of self-examination that the only path to true happiness lies in authenticity.

"The question wasn't whether I should come out, but whether I wanted the fullness of life that comes with authenticity, with expressing my needs and desires, giving myself permission to live them and asking that they be fulfilled. It was a scary process. I wondered what would happen with our clients and other people I knew in business, what would happen with family and friends."

"How did everyone react?" she asked.

"They were great. People were so generous with their love. I found so much kindness and acceptance. There was an outpouring of support, people asking, 'How can we be there for you, how can we show up for you?' That really kind of surprised me, but it was a great reminder of a core belief I've had throughout my life: that most people are good.

"Aside from my sexuality, I don't think either of us were happy in the marriage. Divorce felt like a natural path to more authentic living. But I was worried about the kids. I asked the therapist, 'How can I do this to the kids? How can I put them through this just because of mistakes I made in my life?

"And the therapist said, 'Maybe you're asking the wrong question. Maybe the question is how could you *not* show them what authentic living looks like? How could you *not* display to them that when you are off course, you correct it. You show them that when you find yourself on a path that is not the path you wanted or your authentic path, you love yourself enough to give yourself the freedom and permission to correct the course, get on that path, live your authentic self. Life is a continual resetting of that. So maybe the question isn't how could you do this to them, it is how could you not?' That was really insightful and helpful for me."

"Wow," Emily said. "Did it work out that way with your kids?"

"I *think* so," Hill said slowly. "Our kids are happy, and my relationship with their mom is great. I met my husband, Ben, and we're happy. About seven years ago, I got out of the day-to-day management of our businesses and gave myself freedom to design a life exactly the way I want it. Part of that involved moving from Texas up here to Colorado, where we're trying to build, I guess, a life of intention."

"Did you always want to be a businessman?" Emily asked.

"Oh, sure," he said, nodding rapidly. "Even as a kid I had lemonade stands. A friend I made during my mission reminded me recently that he once asked me what I was going to do with my life, and I said, 'I'm going to build Hill Enterprises.' He asked me, 'How are you going to do that?' and I said, 'I don't know, but it is going to happen.' I saw life, the world, and the universe as generous and was confident that if I worked hard, I would be successful.

"I started my first company with my business partner and friend Chade Nelson. We met a man named Rikko Ollervidez, our first client who searches for small businesses that are just getting started and tries to support them. He happened to be my sister's next-door neighbor. As our first client, Rikko helped us start a property management company, which we thought would take a long time to get off the ground, because Chade and I had little experience in managing properties, but Rikko believed in our vision and loved supporting new entrepreneurs. I owe a great deal of our success to Rikko's generosity. That company eventually grew into Spectrum Association Management, which we sold not long ago."

"I'm interested to hear how you think generosity pays off in business," Emily said.

"Let me say first that I get why it can be scary to be generous," Hill said. "The typical business owner will say, 'What if I'm generous and the generosity doesn't come back to me in increased sales or a more productive workforce or whatever?' I have several answers for that.

"First, generosity really does come back around in some shape or form. There's an undeniable energy that exists around generosity. Whether you call it the universe or God or karma, I believe in this energy. Generosity may not come back exactly when you expect it to or how you expect it to, but it will always come back in some way. I feel that so strongly that even when I have had times of worrying or wondering how some act of generosity would come back to me, I just knew that it would—and it did.

> "There's an undeniable energy that exists around generosity. Whether you call it the universe or God or karma, I believe in this energy."

"Second, lack of generosity will come back around too. Companies that put strict rules for management and employees above human interaction, companies that don't allow management the opportunity and latitude to reward good work, are going to suffer. Young people are asking that question a lot: 'If I'm just a number in this large corporation, what is the point?'

"If you're part of upper management in such a company, you're bringing an ethos of scarcity to your position, no matter how much money you make or how much profit the company makes. When you look in the mirror every morning, do you want to see a generous person, a person who lives with abundance, or a person who lives with scarcity?

"Third, generosity just feels good. It makes you happy, and that's worth a lot. I think generosity in its truest form has little to do with how the receiver behaves or reacts to your generous gift or action. It has more to do with your spirit of giving. It's most rewarding when we let go of the scariness and set ourselves free to give because we want to no matter what the response is."

"Can't generosity make you look weak or like a soft touch?" Emily asked.

"Yes, I suppose it can turn around and bite you," Hill replied. "Earlier in my career, we had an employee who came to us and asked for financial help. She said her power was about to be shut off. She didn't have enough money to pay the bill, and she asked us to pay it. I'd never been asked for money like that before, but I told her we'd pay her electric bill. We did, and she quit a week later.

"That was a blow, but I didn't let it change the way I do business. As leaders of companies, we have to fight against becoming jaded when it comes to generosity. There will be setbacks, and there will be the temptation to live a less generous life or lead in a less generous way. But I can't let one person or even a few people change the way I operate the whole company or how I act every day.

"Generosity doesn't make you a doormat either," Hill continued. "I had a conversation years ago with an employee, a guy right out of college, who came to me wanting a raise because of some need in his life. I explained to him that he'd get the raise sooner than later if he approached his work in a generous way, looking for ways to be the best employee he could be. But if his search was about 'What can you do for me?' and 'I need you to do this for me because I want more money,' he would find fewer raises, fewer opportunities, and less job success.

"As a boss, I always want to reward the individual who is giving authentically, who is generous with their time, generous with their focus, and generous with their effort while they're at work. That is something I would really highlight with a younger person today. And it applies to customers, vendors, and everyone else associated with the company: If you deal with people in an authentic way, you'll be dealt with similarly."

"Interesting," said Emily, remembering all the opportunities Pinafore had given her.

"My loyalty as a leader must never be to the one; it must always be to the whole," Hill said. "And if I'm going to be loyal to the whole, that means that I am going to operate in a generous way, because most people are good. They want to give their best. Most people want to be challenged. Most people want to show up every day and have someone believe in them and ask something of them. So if I can keep being generous, I will keep finding more excellence among my employees. One of the most generous things you can do for people is to believe in them.

"A few years ago, we were in a place where we had a successful company, but we just knew it could do even better and we knew we could increase even more in excellence and generosity. We came across the work of business consultant Cameron Herold and his book *Vivid Vision*. His concept was to conceptualize, in vivid detail, what your company will look like, smell like, taste like, three years from that moment. You map out what the experience will be for every person in your entity: vendors, customers, employees, everybody.

"My business partner and I decided to go all in on this concept. We imagined that as we got larger as an organization, we had to act smaller, with fewer rules and less red tape. We already had a great culture in the company up to that point, but our "vivid vision" pushed it even further. We decided if we really believed in the good in people, if they wanted to do their best and wanted to be challenged, if they wanted to show up every day, then let's work with that instead of punishing the few employees who didn't want to do that.

"So we started giving four weeks of paid time off each year, including the first year. We gave a week of paid volunteer time from day one. We dropped our dress code—I can remember the meeting where people were asking, 'Well, what do we wear?' I answered, 'You're adults, you know what's appropriate. I think you should decide, not me.' If we hired someone who didn't know what to wear, that was on us; we missed the mark. We gave power back to employees in a lot of different ways. Our message was 'We believe you want to give your best and so we want to give you the best.'

"We rolled out these plans to all our offices, and I thought, *You know, I am either going to have major egg on my face in three years, or this will work out.* We knew that we couldn't accomplish it with the team we had that day. But once again, the universe was kind: The day we rolled out the new perks, a guy named Henrik started for us.

"He had the brains and background to implement every single thing we wanted to do. He created hundreds of action points and systematically made our vision happen. He's now the CEO of all of our companies. We were rewarded for our generosity: We handed out a lot of perks, not knowing how it would all work, and the guy who could execute it started that day."

"But if you relax too much, don't you lose control?" Emily asked.

"Generosity cannot be found in control," Hill said firmly. "I get it—it's human nature to try to control an outcome, and especially for companies to legislate every behavior and action. And I understand the need to impose order. There has to be a process and there have to be policies, but when we stop believing in the generous spirit of people working there and try to control every aspect of what is going on, I think we lose that energy."

"Generosity cannot be found in control."

"Then how do you retrain someone who *wants* to be generous but doesn't understand how to become generous, who maybe worked in venues that were highly hierarchical or structured, or were at someone's beck and call?" Emily asked.

"Great question," Hill said. "It really goes back further than that, often to childhood. The employee you want to retrain may have grown up in a home with a lack of generosity, where they could find little love, acceptance, or forgiveness of error. They didn't have a parent or a teacher or someone else who modeled generous thinking. My heart aches for people like that. They reach the job market thinking that people are out to get you, the world is against you, the worst thing that can happen is gonna happen. Those are their ingrained thoughts.

"So I think that improving your generosity depends a lot on whether you can take control of your thoughts and adjust them to a different environment. I think (A) generosity starts in the mind and (B) only you can control what you think. So if you really want to be a generous person, you need to shift your belief from negativity to hopefulness, that the world is on your side and good things are going to happen. This takes a lot of effort for some people. They may have to look proactively for ways to be generous each day. If they aren't generous by nature, they may have to practice.

"I would encourage anyone for whom generosity isn't second nature to practice, to perform small acts of kindness at first and get bigger from there. Practicing shouldn't feel overwhelming, and it can't feel like something you can't do, because you're doing it! There's an element of 'Fake it till you make it,' but you aren't really faking it—you're just rechanneling your energy into positive action instead of static, negative thoughts.

> "I would encourage anyone for whom generosity isn't second nature to perform small acts of kindness at first and get bigger from there."

"If you think of this process as practicing, you aren't waiting for someone to wave a magic wand over you. It's more understandable and approachable and accessible. And since generosity makes the giver happy, practicing every day makes you feel good all the time."

Emily was silent after Hill finished. She was thinking about her parents, how you practically had to win a Nobel Prize to get their attention; how surprised they were when she was accepted at Cornell; how her mom said she'd never make it in hotel work because her room was so sloppy. She thought about how she never made much progress with piano lessons because she didn't practice much, but she got pretty good at guitar because she did. She remembered how happy she'd felt when she found out the Mongolian guest was reunited with his winter coat and when the family in Istanbul made their cruise. Emily could also see that what Andy Hill was saying dovetailed nicely with what Will had told her weeks ago. She felt emotional but managed to hold it together.

"What else do you consider to be part of generosity?" she asked, blinking back a small tear.

"Well, going back to a term I used earlier, feeling your essential okayness," Hill said. "I think this concept of okay-ness is really important when we are children; in fact, we're worried about our okay-ness from birth if you think about it. Are we going to get food? Are we going to be loved? Will we have shelter? In adulthood a lack of okay-ness can show up as a lack of generosity because our world is seen as a world of scarcity.

"So now I have to cling on to everything that I can have. Some people go to bed thinking, *I may lose my job tomorrow and not be able to buy food. We could lose our house and have to sleep in the car. My spouse could stop loving me overnight, and I'll never find anyone to love me again.* I think that stems from the primal childhood need for survival that lies within all of us.

"I established my essential okay-ness when I decided to leave the LDS Church and to come out. That allows me to look in the mirror and know that the guy looking back at me is okay. He is enough, and he is fine just the way he is. Ben and I share that with our kids. You know how it is, kids will say something insulting at school or do mean things, and we always ask, 'Does that say something about them or about you?'

"Of course, it says more about them than about you. They're experiencing a scarcity about something that they can't articulate but is very real. But *you* are okay just the way you are. I think one of the most generous things we can do is to view ourselves as enough and trust that what we have to offer the world is worth giving.

"Part of adulthood," he added, "is recognizing that we are competent human beings with the ability to make decisions, so if we remove the personal threat to any decision we are making for ourselves, we realize it is okay. Often we don't allow ourselves permission to do things we want to do or be the person we want to be for fear of consequences, but the reality is, we are going to be okay. Most of us are thriving individuals, and we will figure out a way to make it work. It might not be fun or enjoyable, but we are going to be okay no matter what happens. When you grasp this concept of okay-ness, you can do anything that seems life-affirming to you, even if there are some negative consequences. You are going to be okay, you are going to live, despite your lizard brain's cries of danger."

Hmm, Emily thought. *Am I okay? Can I make decisions? I haven't really made a job decision since I started at Pinafore. I got promoted, I got sent from one hotel to another, I got assigned this project. I don't buy new clothes unless I have to replace a suit. I've never decorated any place I've lived since Cornell.*

"Another facet of generosity," Hill was saying, "is acceptance of people, not being judgmental about them. I remember vividly the moment I let go of judgment and realized there was a whole other layer of generosity that could be received and given by consciously trying to dissolve judgment in my life.

"This was during my process of coming out, so I was worried about acceptance and being judged, and I was aware that I had judged other people. I was leaving the parking lot of our office, and I saw this car go down the road that was covered in bumper stickers, just covered. You couldn't see the paint anymore. And my first thought was *Wow, that car is so weird! Why would someone ruin a car like that?*

"Then I caught myself. I was judging the car's owner according to what I'd been taught a car should look like. Something in my mind shifted, and I thought *You know, that guy is the coolest person ever. I wish I could meet him. He doesn't care what anyone thinks. I want to hear his story and find out what the stickers represent.* In that moment, I realized that I didn't need to worry about what other people were doing as long as they weren't hurting anyone. I didn't need to worry whether someone else's choice was right or wrong according to my beliefs.

"My judgment shifted to a generous view: I don't know why that person is doing what they're doing, but I bet there is a good reason that I don't understand yet. That attitude has caused me to meet some phenomenal people whom I would have prevented myself from meeting before. That sense of acceptance brought love, perspective, and joy into my life. It became part of my process of coming out.

"I'm convinced that it helped me find acceptance among people in the business community and in the church. Because they saw that I met their reservations with generosity and not judgment and seemed to be comfortable in my own skin, they were able to approach me with greater openness and more acceptance than they might have."

I bet he had a more difficult time than he's letting on, Emily thought. *But what a story and incredible insights.*

"So many people in our country and our world are at each other's throats," Hill mused. "If they were more generous with acceptance, that would change everything. We would all listen to one another, get to know each other, understand the other person's perspective, and walk around in their shoes. Once you do, your heart will go out to that person, and you'll want to help them in ways they want to be helped, and vice versa."

"You're talking about empathy," Emily said. Hill nodded. *I wanted to walk in the guests' shoes*, Emily said to herself, *when I should have been walking in the housekeepers'.*

"Then again," Hill said, "I think generosity requires vulnerability and risk. It is a bit of jumping off the high dive with the confidence that there is going to be something to catch you there. But when you do jump off the high dive of generosity, I think you'll find this incredible universe that is open to you.

"The universe wants to be generous with us. It wants to provide us with a rewarding and enjoyable life. There are going to be trials and struggles. We will have setbacks. But I deeply believe in the generosity of the universe, this energy that wants us to succeed, be happy, and enjoy our existence. If we're willing to jump off that diving board, that other person, whether in a relationship, a friendship, or a work situation, will be there to assist us after we hit the water. If you're courageous enough to put out abundant generosity, I believe you will find abundant generosity."

> **"If you're courageous enough to put out abundant generosity, I believe you will find abundant generosity."**

"Yes, but that takes a real leap of faith," Emily replied. "What if you grew up without anybody there for you? Can you trust that someone will catch you when you fall?"

"Maybe the past isn't that relevant and what counts is the present and the future," Hill shrugged. "My therapist uses this concept of a hard drive. There's nothing on it when you are born, but when we start growing up and becoming aware, files start to accumulate. We interact with our siblings and parents and grandparents. Our teachers show us one attitude or another and get to judge us on every report card. Friends, fellow students, people in church or in the community say things about us, and subconsciously we decide along the way what is true about us and what is BS. It goes onto our hard drive and gets stored as memory.

"Then, as adults, we start to live what we took in as children and carry it out. But that can really hold you back. I think one of the most generous things you can do for yourself is to erase the hard drive, get rid of what other people thought of you, and decide for yourself who you are."

"I think that's easier said than done," Emily argued. "I took developmental psych in college, and the textbook and the professor made a big deal about our experiences in childhood, back to when we're babies. Can you really just wipe the slate clean?"

"Maybe not completely, but if you had bad experiences or bad influences growing up, it's healthy to put that stuff aside," Hill said. "Let's try another metaphor from my therapist, Randal Porter, that focuses on the present. We sit through life facing a huge set of bleachers that are filled with all sorts of people we invited into the ballpark. And all those people are deciding whether every action we take is good or ill-advised, whether they can approve the way we live and even who we are. In other words, they judge our okay-ness—without consulting us.

"I think one of the most generous things we can do for ourselves is to *fire the crowd in the bleachers*. Give them pink slips and tell them, 'You don't get to decide anymore whether I am okay; I do,' so that when you look in the mirror, you aren't seeing all these other people. You're seeing your authentic self, and that self is just fine."

"Okay," Emily nodded, "but even if I can get rid of the naysayers, what if I come from a background that didn't provide a lot of the skills you need for the professional world?" Emily was thinking of a couple of prospective employees she hadn't hired in San Diego because they didn't dress right or seem to know how to talk to guests and co-workers.

"If you arrived at adulthood having never been shown how to navigate a system, even if you never were given an opportunity to develop soft skills or learn how to turn a 'no' into a 'yes,' there are people willing and able to teach you those skills," Hill said. "It might take time, but they will help you, and you will get it done. I think this may be what you are considering doing.

"Imagine that you lived in an isolated little cave your whole life, one that didn't allow you to stand up straight. So when you finally left the cave, you didn't know how to stand up straight, because no one had ever shown you how. You would keep walking hunched over until someone came and showed you how to walk standing straight, and by the way, it's going to feel a lot better. *That person always shows up*, because we live in a world of generous people.

"Generosity is what shows you that the goals you thought were impossible are in fact possible, because generous people will help you along the way. Generosity plays into asking for your needs to be met because you're confident that someone will meet them. Sure, it would be nice if people could figure out your needs through telepathy, but the world doesn't work that way.

"Generosity means keeping at arm's length, if not actually detaching yourself from, everybody who didn't think you had what it takes. Belief in generosity is having faith that there will *always* be someone to teach you and somebody to catch you when you fall. And generosity is something you practice until you get it right, and when you do get it right, you pass it on and do all the things that generous people do."

Emily's head was spinning, but she did some surreptitious deep breathing and slowed down her brain and heart rate. She felt cleaner, somehow, and more confident that she could join, and maybe lead, in the world of the generous.

"Thank you, Andy," she said, getting up. "You've been a terrific interview subject, and I've learned a lot today."

"My pleasure," Hill said. "Let me know if there's anything you need in the future."

As Emily walked back to her car, she realized at that moment that *she* was okay, that actually she had worked out her essential okay-ness in college. Up until then she'd lived with parents who always made her feel that her best wasn't quite good enough and her failings would be huge obstacles to her progress. Emily had been surprised to get into Cornell too. Her grades in high school were great, but not top of her class, and she'd done the bare minimum of community service.

But she *had* been accepted, and she put in lots of hours and did excellent work in school. She got involved in more activities and made lots of friends. By the time she graduated, new job at Pinafore Global in hand, she felt she was doing just fine. *Don must have recognized my okay-ness in that mission statement he liked so much,* Emily thought.

That mission statement somehow got buried under mountains of business magazines and hours of social media. Emily remembered how impressed she'd been with the wealthy, beautifully dressed people who stayed at Pinafore hotels. Some of them would snap their fingers—sometimes literally—and multiple assistants would appear to carry out their wishes. For a long time, Emily thought their lives were what she should aspire to.

Not anymore.

Emily got in her rental car and, by habit, drove around the corner so Hill wouldn't see her sitting in the car and come out to ask if anything was wrong. After she pulled over, she took out her phone to send Don a text. Her message was exactly four words:

I get it now.

CHAPTER 13

OH, BEHAVE: CHRISTOPHER GRAVES

There's something about this place, Emily reflected, standing in the sun and breathing the warm morning air. *It feels such a part of our history, but it's so contemporary at the same time.* She was back in Washington, DC, this time near Dupont Circle, standing on the sidewalk in front of a row of venerable townhouses. She looked up and down the street at the stately houses; it was the first time in America that she'd seen really old buildings people actually lived in. *This street makes Old Town San Diego look like a movie set,* Emily thought.

She wanted to use the knocker on the front door—it seemed only appropriate—but noticed the Ring doorbell and figured Christopher Graves would want to see who was at the door. He answered quickly, a gray-haired man in his sixties, wearing all black: a black long-sleeve T-shirt, black slim jeans, and black Hoka sneakers. Like most of her interview subjects, Graves exuded warmth and welcome.

"Mr. Graves, hello," Emily said.

"Chris, please," he said. "And you're Emily."

"Yes," Emily said, smiling. She'd started her first meetings of the project with a neutral, businesslike face, but by the end of the summer, she'd noticed that her interview subjects all greeted her smiling, and she'd begun to mirror their expressions, even subconsciously.

"Please come in." Emily entered a large, light-filled living room with a high ceiling and big, sun-filled windows. It featured modern seating, but the side tables looked like antiques and the art was clearly Asian.

"This is where I set up for Zoom, but most of the time I work in the kitchen, in a little nook that I designed," Graves said. He ushered her to a small space just off the kitchen, smaller than a walk-in closet but featuring a good-sized window looking out at a patio and well-kept garden. A laptop and some scattered pages sat on a beautiful walnut table. Graves had a modern ergonomic chair, but he'd taken pains to find an old wooden filing cabinet.

"That table is just breathtaking," Emily said.

"Thanks," Graves replied. "I had it made for me. This is where I spend most of my time. I'd probably get more work done if I sat with my back to the window, but I'd miss a lot of entertainment. There are a pair of doves who visit every day, and a couple of rambunctious squirrels who root through our pots of herbs looking for food and who chatter angrily at me because I didn't leave them a nut to grab."

"This house must be more than a hundred years old," Emily said as they went back to the living room.

"Oh, much more," Graves said. "It dates from 1891. I really like living here, especially now that I work from home most of the time. The walls are very thick, so it's quiet, but all the houses are attached to one another, so you also get a feeling of connection.

"I'm a lot more introverted now than I was three years ago. I actually get irritated if I don't have dedicated time where I'm just reading, writing, and thinking. It is not being antisocial so much as a gift of introspection, which I probably didn't have as strongly before the pandemic. Back then, you would just as easily have found me on a plane as in an office—that's how much traveling I did. I love working from home. It's a lot more comfortable than the many offices at Ogilvy that I've been in over thirty years. I've probably been in ninety of our hundred offices around the world. That's probably how I got to know Don in so many places."

"And he says hi and thank you very much," Emily said. "You have some amazing art objects," she added, gazing around the thoughtfully curated space.

"These things around the room come from the places where we lived around the world for sixteen years. We lived in Asia for twelve years and in Europe for four. We have Islamic art from Turkey next to pictures of me and our two kids in Switzerland, and then there's some Japanese pottery. My wife and kids and I were very fortunate to live among different cultures for so long."

I lived in Hong Kong, Istanbul, and Brussels, and I didn't bring home a single souvenir, Emily thought. *What does that say about me?*

"What were your early years like?" she asked.

"I grew up in a very low-income housing project in Norfolk, Virginia. It could be a violent place; I quit a paper route at twelve after I was robbed at gunpoint," Graves said. "I was the youngest of five children, so there were seven of us in what was probably a five-hundred-square-foot cinderblock box. It didn't have sheetrock on the inside, so you could see the walls sweat. I didn't envy middle-class or wealthy kids, though, because I didn't know any.

"Along came Mrs. Davis, a third-grade teacher, who talked an old, very prestigious private school, Norfolk Academy, into giving me a scholarship. My parents, who were from New England, were all for it."

"Very fortunate, but that must have been something of a culture shock," Emily observed.

"It certainly was," Graves agreed. "I was lucky to go to Norfolk Academy, but it made me aware that there were kids who came from a world of privilege I still didn't have access to. I actually hid from them where I lived and walked a mile and a half to the other side of the interstate outside the projects. When the school bus picked me up, the other students couldn't see where I lived, and I tried desperately to keep that secret. Years later, some people from my class asked me if I'd really lived in the projects, and for the first time, I told them that I did—I'd been too scared to share that when we were in school. There was friction at home, too, because when you meet kids who have what you don't have, your expectations rise about what you should have.

"But then I got even luckier, if you want to call it that: I was offered a full ride at Phillips Exeter Academy in New Hampshire," Graves said. "A man named Harvard Knowles, a Melville scholar who started teaching at Exeter the same year I started as a student there, helped me so much. He was a terrifically empathetic person who understood how it felt when the rich kids pushed my buttons, and he'd swoop in before I did something dumb or self-destructive, something that would get me kicked out because of bad behavior or a bad attitude. He would do it not by lecturing but by being a kind questioner, asking smart questions that made you think a bit more."

"He sounds like a great guy," Emily said.

"Here's an illustration. My mother was in her eighties when she finally saw Exeter. My father didn't work while I was growing up, and my mother raised five kids as a nurse whose salary topped out at $30,000. I know you're here to learn about generosity; she was the one who was perhaps the most generous of anybody in my life, because she never kept a penny to herself for anything. I took her up there in the summer because Harvard Knowles was teaching a class on *Moby-Dick*. I love that novel because Melville weaves a tapestry that tells the story of America. It isn't just a long book about a guy who wants to catch a whale.

"Mom was nervous about sitting in on Harvard's seminar because she went to nursing school, not college, and she felt insecure about these eggheads sitting around the table analyzing Melville. Even I started to get a little squeamish about how my former teacher was going to view my mother. But when Mom arrived, Harvard asked her to come sit next to him, and he made sure she felt welcome and her views appreciated.

"That's why I stayed close to Harvard Knowles over the years, because he had such a remarkable way of generosity that emanated from him. People like him and like Mrs. Davis really changed the trajectory of what could have been an extremely sad, banal, anonymous life."

"Where did you go for college?" Emily asked.

"I got my undergraduate degree at Wesleyan University, and after I graduated, I was a TV producer for a bunch of different broadcasts," Graves said. "Then I worked for Dow Jones (*The Wall Street Journal*) for eighteen years. In 2005, I went to work for Ogilvy, which was best known as a Madison Avenue advertising agency after its founding in 1948 but now employs about fifteen thousand people in a hundred offices around the world.

"Ogilvy had been divided into three vertical companies globally: Ogilvy Public Relations, Ogilvy Advertising, and one called Ogilvy One (now we call it Experience), which was about digital and Internet stuff. I was brought on as CEO for the public relations operation in Asia, called Asia Pacific, where we developed all of our behavioral science work as a sort of side hustle. Then I was promoted and became the global CEO for Ogilvy Public Relations. About six years ago, behavioral science, which is the study of human actions, became the center of my life when I won a Rockefeller Foundation Fellowship.

"It's called the Bellagio Residency. Very tough gig," Graves said sardonically. "They put you in a sixteenth-century villa on the shores of Lake Como in Italy. There are thirteen people in the house. Picture a 'save the world' reality show, where they have thirteen people connected to behavioral science living together for a month. It's a combination of absolute quiet and debate, so you come together at every meal, in the evening you have discussions and debates about huge things, and then you retreat into your own room or workspace to write, reflect, and read for the rest of the time."

"I'm sorry, but that sounds like the most boring reality show ever," Emily said, smiling.

"Oh, definitely," Graves agreed, "but it gave me confidence that I actually knew something about behavioral science, and I was able to overcome a kind of imposter syndrome about working in it full-time. When I got home, I started what we call the Ogilvy Center for Behavioral Science, and that community has grown. We now have CEOs for Asia, Europe, and North America for behavioral science, which encompasses a lot of disciplines, including economics, law, psychology, and illness, and work across an entire spectrum of projects. I do a lot of work in public health–related behavioral science on topics like the Covid pandemic and climate change. For example, I work with FEMA on a project involving the communication of climate change mitigation using behavioral science.

"We work with near-insolvable problems, so you have to have enough resilience that if you see small incremental gains, you're happy with that. You go in knowing that you aren't suddenly going to cure vaccine hesitancy and you are not going to completely flip attitudes related to climate change. You try to adjust your expectations about impact and play the long game: that very small impacts sometimes cascade into a very large impact if increasing numbers of people get on board."

"How does behavioral science tie in with generosity?"

"A lot of us realize as we mature that generous actions feel good."

"Well, a lot of us realize as we mature that generous actions feel good. Rarely, I think, are people disappointed by helping or sharing. And if they *are* disappointed, for example if they feel that the people they shared with ignored or exploited their generosity, they don't stay that way, because we're wired to remember good experiences and forget the negative ones."

"Really?" Emily said. "Don't people feel bad when their good deeds get ignored, or the object of their generosity takes advantage of them, or they're even punished for the good thing they've done?" *And don't people carry grudges anymore?* she thought.

"I'm only disappointed in one scenario," Graves said. "When someone I haven't seen for a while gets in touch and wants to meet transactionally. You meet, and I say, 'Hey, how have you been, how are your kids?' and the person doesn't want to talk about their family. They're only interested in what I can do for them: they or their kid needs a recommendation, they want to do business with you, they need start-up capital. If I can, I do what they want me to do, or I refer them to someone else, but I think, okay, this is transactional. And even if what someone wants doesn't cost money, it takes time from my work.

"I find most people to be either more transactional in their interactions with other people—that is, if they do something for someone, they expect something in return—or relational, which means they

help or share things with people for its own sake and form relationships that transcend any mutual benefit."

Emily thought back to many of the transactional interactions she
had initiated—and winced inside.

"In hiring, especially for a management position, I now do a small
test," Graves continued. "I say, 'Tell me about two, three, or four people
whom you have not worked with for a long time, who worked with you
or for you, and tell me what they are doing now.'

"The people who struggle, who think it an odd question, thought of
people in a shallow, transactional way. They considered people only in
the present, those who could do something for them. The others, who
are more relationship-oriented, start telling you anecdotes of how they
just caught up with someone after twenty years or how they stay in
touch with former colleagues."

I'm glad I never had to take that test, Emily thought. *I barely keep up with
friends.*

"I also say 'yes' a lot. It doesn't cost me very much, and I've found the
return to be generous to others and myself. Every day or every other
day, someone I know says to me, 'Chris, I think this person would really
get something out of meeting you. Would you have coffee with them?'
I generally say yes. I know that some of these people might be transactional—for example, they're seeking a job at Ogilvy—but others aren't.
They're just looking to talk things out with someone who knows the
work world because they are a little lost at the moment, or they are
looking for encouragement to confirm a decision they are thinking of
making. I've never been disappointed in meetings like that because,
for one thing, you usually end up learning something from them, or,
even better, you strike up a relationship with the person, you have the
feeling that the two of you should meet again. What could be a one-off
turns into an ongoing give-and-take."

> **"I say 'yes' a lot. It doesn't cost me very much, and I've found the return to be generous to others and myself."**

"That must take a lot of your time too," Emily said.

"Yes, but I haven't been disappointed by the nuggets that emerge in these conversations," Graves said. "But you're right, Emily, I lose all self-discipline when I meet with interesting people. I say to myself, *I am going to stick to forty-five minutes this time*, and suddenly it's three hours later. Even worse, that poor person probably wanted to leave after forty-five minutes and here we've been, just talking and talking. But I get caught up in the moment when I'm sharing with someone and both of us are willing to show a little vulnerability. Neither of us is selling to the other person or trying to get the other to think of them in a certain frame. People can be remarkably interesting when they are in that mode rather than a transactional mode.

"Here's a good example. I was on the board of a great charity for about twelve or fourteen years. We built and managed twenty-one schools in Cambodia, finding and training teachers and helping children attend and stay in school—seven thousand of them. Bill and Jamie Amelio, who founded the organization, invited me onto the board because I might have ideas about helping them with the psychology of fundraising and other aspects of running the organization. Sure, they wanted something from me, my ideas and whatever expertise I had to offer, but they wanted me for *me*, because I'd lived in Asia and cared about education. They weren't tapping me because they thought I was a rich guy who could hemorrhage money."

"Fundraising psychology. Fascinating. How much attention do you give to what some people call the science of generosity?"

"Oh, the neuroscientists have that all figured out," Graves said. "They know which neurotransmitters and hormones make you feel good and what parts of the brain they affect.

"Psychologists and neuroscientists also have identified cognitive biases that either impede generosity or can drive it, in all or some of its forms. A lot of factors determine how generous you are. For example, you might be influenced by what other people are doing—the social norms of your community or workplace or house of worship. Even if you are not naturally altruistic, you look at the behaviors around you, and if giving is an expected behavior, you tend to comply with that, at least a little. In personality trait theory, there are five basic human traits, and one of the traits is agreeableness. People who are higher in agreeableness tend to be more generous than people who are critical of everything.

"Adam Grant, who has written several books about workplace dynamics and teaches organizational psychology at the Wharton School of Business, says most people, 56 percent, are 'matchers.' These folks take their cues from how they're treated, and they reciprocate in kind. If you are mean to them, they will be mean to you, and if you are nice to them, they'll be nice to you. Although 'matching' behavior is more or less transactional—'I'll give you what you give me'—matchers have the propensity to show generous behavior if they are mirroring the generosity of the people they deal with. That's very different from the 'takers,' who not only are interested in what people can do for them but seek to give back as little as they can, and the 'givers,' who share whatever they can without concern for what they get in return.

"There's also something called 'locus of control,' which is the degree to which people believe that they, as opposed to external forces, have control over the outcome of events in their lives. In other words, do you believe that you control your destiny, or do external forces such as fate, God, or powerful people control it? People whose locus of control is internal are more generous than people who are wired to think that something or someone else is pulling their strings. They believe their own actions determine how they feel, so they tend to do things for themselves and others that will produce satisfaction.

"Then there's 'regulatory focus,' which is about whether you make decisions that will push yourself forward or decisions made to avoid failure or harm. The person with a 'promotion focus' is always trying to reach the next level, even if their actions bring risk of failure: think athletes such as Rafael Nadal or Steph Curry, who are always going for the point. The person with a 'prevention focus' is someone who wants to just keep the ball in play until someone makes a mistake. One group is not more generous than the other, but they have different motivations for giving, whether it be time, money, or mentorship. The promotion-focused person likes to see the change in someone's life that their action brings; these are people participating in job-training or school programs. Prevention-focused people are more motivated by mitigating or avoiding harm in another person's life, so they're more likely to volunteer at food banks and shelters for the unhoused."

"I'm learning a lot today," murmured Emily, scribbling furiously in her notebook. Looking up, she asked, "What else leads people to be generous?"

"Well, it's important to understand how humans connect to one another. Particularly as we move to a more digital and AI world, human intelligence and the shared human experience become more important. For example, there is something called the 'identifiable victim effect.' The idea is that humans maximize their empathy or sympathy when they can imagine the plight of one single individual. The empathy decreases when the focus is on a group: a population or even a family rather than a single person. Psychologists will say that humans have a very shallow empathy pool. But it drives home the power of relating to another person.

"As we move to a more digital and AI world, human intelligence
and the shared human experience become more important."

"A great example of the identifiable victim effect was the two-year-old Syrian refugee child, Aylan Kurdi, who drowned. Before he died, along with his mother and brother, there was a lot of press about Syrian refugees, what they went through, how they died, and frankly, not many people in this country cared. But somebody photographed Aylan lying face down on the beach, and that one picture of one child was in every newspaper, on every news broadcast, and on every news website the next day. The picture doubled the number of Internet searches about Syrian refugees, and it caused a rise in donations to refugee organizations. If you want someone to truly care about another, you don't talk in abstractions or about a large population; you try to embody the problem in one single individual. Just like how we engage more deeply in one-on-one conversations than big group lectures. It's really a biggie in triggering generosity."

"So, what impedes how we connect to one another?"

"What gets in the way is something called psychological distance, which operates in several dimensions," Graves said. "The first is *time*— the further away from the present something happened or will happen, the less people care about it. A lot of people see climate change as something that will affect us in the distant future and say, 'Well, I'll worry about it when we get there.' Or if someone tries to explain that slavery has had an effect on many contemporary American institutions, they'll say, 'Oh, but slavery ended more than a hundred and fifty years ago.'

"The second dimension is *physical* distance. If there's a situation on the other side of the planet, people don't attach as much because it's so far away. Americans are horrified by widespread wildfires in California and Oregon but less so when similar wildfires devour forests in Australia.

"And the third form of distance is *social*: Are the people like me or unlike me? The more unlike me, the less I connect as a human being. We've seen this with people thrown out of Myanmar and China, for example. Not many Americans feel a close personal relationship with people in those regions. But when Russia attacked Ukraine, there was an outpouring of support from a large segment of this country, because they have significant communities in America, and as such we more closely relate to them.

"In general, most people want to see something as vivid and concrete, versus high level and abstract," Graves said. "The more high level and abstract something is, the less people bond to it emotionally. Therefore, to truly give of oneself you need to relate and be emotionally engaged."

> **"To truly give of oneself you need to relate and be emotionally engaged."**

"So what has your center come up with since it was established?"

"A few years ago, a partner and I put together what we call 'the real why and the hidden who.' Our goal was to show how personality traits, cultural understanding, and cognitive styles reveal aspects of individuals that either drive behavioral change or serve as barriers to it. In the world of branding and marketing, knowledge of the 'real why'—why people do what they do, even if they don't know the reason themselves—helps marketers understand consumers' real motivations for buying some products and not others. And being able to identify someone's 'hidden who'—to look beneath surface demographics and understand who an individual really is—offers a way to reach consumers that is based on empathy."

"How does generosity figure in this context?" Emily asked.

"Humans by and large are more generous if they can identify with the other person. Unfortunately, no matter what domain I'm working in—climate change, vaccines, countering disinformation—we are reminded again and again about the evolutionary power and *deleterious* effects of identity. It's a strong, bonding glue between some populations, but it can be the biggest source of repulsion with others. The tendency to be generous to people who we think are like us is hardwired, inherent, for most of us.

"Add to that the components of the real why and the hidden who. We don't all start at the same place. For example, one of the five major personality traits besides agreeableness is openness to experience. Someone might be on the low end of that spectrum, consistent and cautious, and might come from a small world of identity affinity, where they don't trust people outside their group. It's going to be difficult to persuade that person to be generous to someone who isn't from that world and doesn't look like anyone they know. It isn't impossible, but it is more of a challenge.

"That said, it's also risky to assign specific traits to broad categories of people. There are, for example, generations shaped by collective experience. So you might find similarities among Americans who lived through the Depression or World War II. You could say that people who were students during the pandemic went through a collective experience. But you're painting with too broad a brush if you categorize all members of Gen Z as being alike. They come from too many backgrounds, and there are too many permutations of how they're wired. Marketers want to be able to appeal to the 'average' millennial, but that person doesn't exist. You just can't say that all Gen Z people are lazy and obsessed with their smart-phones. There are too many who aren't."

Emily, who had long considered herself different from others in her age cohort, nodded in agreement.

"It's really amazing how little we as human beings have changed over the centuries. We've never been wired to think long term, for example. That made sense in the days of hunter-gatherers, when people lived from day to day and usually died by age fifty, but modern humans need to make plans, like save for a retirement that could run forty years. Focusing on identity was understandable when people rarely left their villages, and a group of folks you didn't know could easily pose a threat, but it doesn't make sense now, when most of us live in cities and suburbs and see all kinds of people who don't look like us. It boggles the mind that, as a species, so many of us are still triggered by things that are ancient in our evolution but no longer applicable. Identity and urgency are two things that you would think we'd have overcome by now."

"Hmm... What exactly does that mean for generosity?" Emily asked, now feeling a little overwhelmed by all the information.

"I guess...don't expect to change humans, certainly not as a species, and very little as individuals. Although it's possible to decode them so you can understand their seemingly irrational behavior," Graves said with a grin.

"If you are trying to encourage prosocial behaviors, which gener-osity is, understand that not everybody is wired to be prosocial. Much of the time you are really going up against some very strong hidden internal wiring."

"Does that mean you don't think someone can become generous who isn't hardwired for it?" Emily asked, a bit anxiously.

"I wouldn't go that far, but I think we should view generosity as a behavior, not as a character trait. That means people can become more generous one act at a time, a learned behavior. But you cannot convince anyone to become more generous by making them feel bad. Eventually someone may become a generous person, that *can* become their character, but only after internalizing many acts of kindness and embracing the behavior as important in their life.

"I try to make generosity attractive by reminding people of the reward they'll get: 'You are going to benefit in ways that may not show up right away. But you will benefit, in ways you can't imagine.' It is the act itself that will help others and make you feel good. Accordingly, we should focus on the behavior—not whether someone is inherently generous but whether they are doing acts of generosity. That means everybody is eligible."

"You're the first person I've interviewed who has explained this to me in behavioral terms," Emily said.

"I'm surprised, because the evidence is compelling," Graves said. "The moment you characterize somebody, you create tribal lines, but if you try to influence what that person *does*, rather than what they're like or not like, you can make some headway. You can make all the choices theirs: the specific action, the motive, the depth of involvement. The person who helps may expect a shot of dopamine or some favor in the future or nothing at all. To me it doesn't matter; the act is the same.

"A lot of people think you have to change someone's mind before you can change their behavior, but behavioral scientists have found that the opposite is true: Behavior change comes first, and eventually belief will follow. Suppose you convince someone to start recycling, just separating out the recyclable trash and putting it in the blue bin every week. It may take ten years, but the act of recycling is likely to make the recycler more environmentally empathetic, even if they weren't when they started that behavior.

"It's much more effective and a lot easier to get people to adopt prosocial behaviors than it is to lecture, moralize, and threaten in hopes of changing minds."

Graves promised to share some materials he and his colleagues had worked on, as well as findings from researchers and experts in behavioral science, as soon as he had time to sort through what would be the most helpful to Emily on this quest.

How's that for generosity? she thought, looking forward to all the interesting insights that would be waiting in her inbox.

As Emily walked back toward Dupont Circle, she kept repeating *everybody is eligible* to herself, and her head was swimming with psychological jargon. *What were the other three personality traits, and where did she fall on the spectrum of each one? Was her locus of control internal or external?* She wanted to think she controlled her destiny, but it certainly felt as if Don had been pulling the strings for a while. Maybe her personality type had changed from five years ago. Had she been transactional in her relationships, and if she had, could she change that?

Emily quickened her pace to her hotel. She was about to spend a lot of time in front of her laptop and couldn't wait to get there.

CHAPTER 14

HIGHER CALL:
MELISSA DAWN SIMKINS

It had been a strenuous ride from Dulles, although Ashburn, Virginia, was pretty close to the airport. Emily knew from her research that the population of Loudoun County had increased tenfold in the past twenty years, but she wasn't prepared for the tenfold increase in traffic. *Sheesh, if it's like this midmorning, I'd hate to see it at 5:00 p.m.*, she thought. It was high summer in northern Virginia, and Emily wondered if she would drive under the kind of leafy trees they didn't have in San Diego, but once she was off the highway, she saw industrial buildings and newer-looking apartment complexes dotted with saplings, their leaves wilting under the bright sun.

Finally, Emily reached the home of Melissa Dawn Simkins, a motivational speaker, author, and expert in branding. The house was large but definitely was built before the population boom.

Emily walked to the front door, feeling her hair frizz from the humidity with every step.

Simkins opened the door for Emily with a big smile that put her more at ease. To Emily's surprise, Simkins handed her a little book with blank pages, a journal.

"This is for you," Simkins said.

"Thank you," said Emily. "This is very nice of you."

"I'm a gift-giver," Simkins said, shrugging. "Come on into my home office."

Simkins was a sleek, beautiful woman who had to be in her forties—her book about branding had been published fifteen years ago—but didn't look it, with an unlined face and a waterfall of dark, streaked hair that seemed unaffected by the humidity outside. The office, just off the entryway, was just as streamlined and lovely, with tasteful furniture, recessed lighting, and a candle glowing next to the desk.

"What a nice room," Emily said.

Simkins thanked her and indicated for her to sit in an overstuffed chair, part of a conversation corner. After some small talk, they got started with the interview.

"Would you tell me about how you grew up?" Emily asked.

"My childhood was very multidimensional," Simkins said. "When I started kindergarten in small-town Indiana, my sister and I were the only two Black children in the school, but my mother taught me how to see my classroom as a flower garden.

"When I came back home from that first day at school, I was upset. No one even let us sit down on the bus. The other children in kindergarten had looked at me as if I were from another planet. My mom saw that I was upset and asked me why, and when I told her, she took out a big piece of white paper and our watercolors, and she showed me how to paint a flower garden. We spent a long time painting flowers, all different colors. When we finished, it was just beautiful.

"Mom said, 'You know, this flower garden we just made is like God's flower garden, because God made flowers of every color you can think of. They're all different, but they all represent beauty. God did the same thing with people: Everyone is a different color, but they're all beautiful in different ways. Not all people will recognize your beauty, and you may not see all of their beauty, but when you look at your classmates tomorrow, I want you to remember this flower garden we just made.'

"That was one of my first lessons in generosity that involved ideas and not just having or sharing stuff. It was a wonderful lesson."

"Very powerful," Emily murmured. "What took your family to a small town in Indiana?"

"My dad is from Gary, Indiana, the first one in his family to go to college. We were in a small town because he was getting his PhD. My parents were very earthy people—well, really, they were hippies. We would eat natural food and granola before either of them was a thing. Mom put sprouts on my sandwiches. It was very odd for a Black family to eat like that, but I didn't know that until we moved to the South.

"Back in the seventies, my parents often would bring people into our home. The former drummer for John Cougar Mellencamp lived with us for like six months. He ate the same stuff my parents did and taught me how to make seed burgers. Another time my parents took in a woman and her daughter; the mom had been abused by her husband. My folks always opened their home to help people. They were very generous in sharing our lives to help people in hard times.

"Dad finished his degree and got his first teaching job in North Carolina, so we moved down there, to a small city called Fayetteville, not much more than an hour south of Raleigh. That's where I formed my identity, so I think of myself as a Southern girl. Fayetteville is a military town, and I went to *the* best high school in the world, E.E. Smith—Go Bulls!—with a lot of kids whose parents were stationed at Fort Bragg."

"That must have been a culture shock," Emily said.

"Oh, you have no idea. But it wasn't going from north to south or from little town to city," Simkins said. "It was going from an environment where my sister and I were the only Black children in school to—well, I'd never seen so many Black people in my life, so many people who looked like me. Some girl who was darker than I am accused me of thinking I was too pretty, you know, that I was conceited, and she wanted to beat me up because I was 'light skinned.' I didn't even know what light skin was. I thought people with light skin were white people.

"The whole dynamic of my identity and not being accepted was really perplexing for me. I came from a place where I was judged just for being Black, and suddenly I was picked on for not being black enough. That really gave me a different perspective on race. I experienced prejudice from both white and Black people, and that's an interesting dynamic at a young age, when you're trying just to figure out who you are.

"I grew up in a world in which white people were always a presence. My parents often were the first Black people in some of the church organizations we were a part of. At the same time, my father taught African American studies, and so he raised me with a great appreciation for African American history. I knew what had happened to my ancestors in America, and it caused me no shame. My unique experience, paired with my spirituality and relationship with God, helped me to see people beyond color."

"That's amazing," Emily said. "In my experience, usually a person has to be biracial to have that perspective."

"Well, we're all a little bit multiracial, aren't we?" Simkins said mischievously.

Emily nodded uncertainly. She'd always thought of herself, for better or worse, as one of the whitest people in any room. She wondered whether Ancestry.com would have anything to say about that.

"Anyway, I loved being a girl in Fayetteville," Simkins said. "Growing up in North Carolina gave me a strong sense of community. It also gave me reassurance that, being a young Black girl, I was special, and I could do great things. I worked on service projects during my teen years, because my church community did them, and eventually I got involved with them on my own. Service became a core part of my identity.

"Also, there were two books that had a big impact on me. One of them was *The Measure of Our Success: A Letter to My Children and Yours* by Marian Wright Edelman, the founder of the Children's Defense Fund. I was only seven or eight when someone gave me her book, but I was always a reader, and I understood what Edelman was saying. She talked about service being the rent you pay for living. My mom and dad would say the same thing: *You gotta pay rent. You gotta get out here and help somebody else. It's not just about you.* They instilled that in us, and so did our community.

"The other book that shaped me was by the Bahamian evangelist Myles Munroe, titled *Understanding Your Purpose.* I got that when I was about fourteen, and it was pivotal. People would always ask you, 'What do you want to be when you grow up?' I didn't know. One day I wanted to be a hairdresser, and the next day I wanted to be a doctor. Munroe challenged me because he insisted I was meant to have one purpose, and my job was to find it. He wanted me to find my 'why,' the reason I was put on Earth, and I'd never really understood what that was about.

"In high school, I started a philanthropic initiative for my high school called REACH—Remember to Extend A Caring Hand, which took on a number of initiatives. We volunteered to work with the elderly, and we also provided mentors to children in the elementary schools. I even showed my community spirit by participating in beauty pageants, spending time growing up in and through pageant work. I was Miss E.E. Smith for my high school and Miss Teen Fayetteville, and service was part of both roles. The thread of generosity started at home, but it wove through my civic, church, and school communities.

> **"The thread of generosity started at home, but it wove through my civic, church, and school communities."**

"When I was in eleventh grade, my dad was offered a professorship at Otterbein University, just outside Columbus, Ohio. I didn't want to leave my high school or my friends, the life I'd made for myself in Fayetteville. But a chance opened for me to stay there. One of my best friends lived down the street from us, and I would go over to her house all the time. I had a set of at least ten adopted aunties and uncles in North Carolina because of her. One day my friend's parents said, 'You know, our older daughter is off at college. Melissa can come live with us.' So my parents and my sister moved to Ohio, and I lived with my Aunt Ruth and Uncle Gene in Fayetteville. Their generosity allowed me to stay and finish high school at E.E. Smith.

"I'm so glad I was able to graduate from Smith. Our principal gladly gave hundreds of hours to the school. We'd get involved in programs to support our community that one of the moms would run during Black History Month. During college spring break, students who had graduated from my high school would come to our classes and tell us what it was like in college and how to get ready. They would give their vacation time to come back to high school and help us understand the big world of college. I knew so many people who gave of themselves to help others.

"So after graduation you rejoined your parents in Ohio."

"That's right," Simkins said. "I did my undergraduate work at Otterbein with help from a community service scholarship. That involved running a community service initiative called the Indianola Mentor Program in inner-city Columbus. My mentoring work there was really a passion project for me; it sort of continued what I did in high school."

"Your generosity and your relationships with generous people go all the way back to when you were a small child, then," Emily said.

"Yes, definitely," Simkins said. "My parents, my friends, the adults in my life, my high school, and my community all modeled generosity for me. I was blessed to have the childhood and adolescence that I had, because I was given gift after gift after gift. I tried to give back a little then, but I'm in a better position to give back now, to fulfill that obligation.

"But I would say the *why* of whatever generosity I've shown is my relationship with God. The giving spirit I demonstrate is rooted in my faith, which of course was also modeled when I was growing up by my parents and other adults, and by my church, where I spent so much time."

"The church you grew up in sounds like a big influence on you," Emily said.

"It was, because a lot of my relationships and my support system came from the church. But the influence went far beyond the church I attended. I was also moved by people who were outside of our church. Even though they didn't go to my church, they still had faith as their core driver for the loving, generous things they did. There's a very strong thread between how spirituality fuels this generosity.

"Sometimes the advice I received was not just spiritual but practical," Simkins continued. "One of the young ladies in my church, who had recently gotten married, took me aside and told me to wait for the right man. I was seventeen, and she wasn't a daughter of my parents' friends, but she took the time to give me the wisdom of the five years or so of experience that she had beyond mine. She said, 'Listen, you're beautiful, you're talented, don't let guys take advantage of you.' Just her taking the time to talk to me and model that generous spirit made me want to be like her, and to think maybe one day I'd find love like she found love. She probably saved me from getting my heart broken by one or two knuckleheaded boys.

"Faith, in my view, goes way beyond any one church. It is rooted in my fundamental belief in Jesus Christ as my Lord and Savior, the belief that He's bigger than this world. He's bigger than any short-term pain that I go through, yet He's with me in those moments of pain, helping me see beyond my current circumstance. Belief is an important and probably the largest piece of my identity."

Emily was impressed by Simkins's fervor. She'd been raised by a mother who thought all religion was BS and a father who called himself a "retired Catholic," so a personal belief in Jesus as savior, let alone a relationship with a church, was alien to her. In fact, she'd had to work hard not to identify anyone with strong spiritual beliefs as a religious fanatic. But as she got older and met more people of many different faiths, Emily found herself fascinated by people who brought together their business interests with their spiritual practices, the ones who conducted business in line with their religious values. Their generosity seemed to flow from the teachings of their faith communities.

"Tell me about how you built your career after you graduated," she said.

"Well, I really got started as an undergraduate," Simkins said. "While I was majoring in public relations at Otterbein, I worked in marketing for the vice president of PR for Victoria's Secret. That's where the branding bug bit me; I learned how powerful branding can be. After college, I worked in marketing for Nationwide Insurance and in sports. I also earned a master's degree in integrated marketing and communications at Northwestern.

"I was doing well in the corporate world, and being my own boss was just a fleeting thought I had from time to time. Then tragedy hit: My boyfriend dropped dead on the basketball court, and my father was diagnosed with cancer. I fell apart and went through a year and a half of depression and loss.

"Finally, I recovered my sense of purpose, and this time it told me to serve the world as an entrepreneur, to turn my passion for people into profit. It took years, but I launched my company, Velvet Suite, from my living room in 2006 with no contacts, contracts, or clients after leaving a global company with a great title and cushy benefits. The purpose of Velvet Suite is to encourage C suite executives and their leadership teams to identify hidden barriers and design solutions for impact. We advise clients on how to present themselves to the marketplace but also in finding and accelerating the promotion of underrepresented talent. In 2007, I wrote a book titled *Brand Me: The Ultimate Playbook for Personal Branding*.

"Velvet Suite's breakthrough came when, in partnership with the NFL, it created the NFL Player Brand University, where for the first time, professional football players could develop personal brands. Since then, Velvet Suite's clients have included Kraft, Boston Scientific, Lincoln Financial, Allstate, Astra Zeneca, Gillette, Procter & Gamble, Home Depot, Southern Company, Oscar Mayer, the NBA, the NCAA, and a number of celebrities and pro athletes. We're helping launch more than three hundred brands!"

"And that's why you're called 'the first lady of personal branding,'" Emily said with a smile.

"Well, yes, but that title didn't come from me," Simkins said, wagging her finger playfully.

"Tell me about She-Suite."

"She-Suite is an initiative, started in 2013, that came out of my work with Velvet Suite. I envisioned a program that would help career-driven, high-potential women discover their purpose and develop paths to leadership. There's an emphasis on lifestyle innovation, to encourage women to create lives they can love. I believe you can brand a beautiful life that includes a great career but doesn't neglect faith, family, wellness, and style."

"Does that mean having it all?" Emily asked. "You know, career, happy marriage, motherhood, good health?"

"I don't see why not, if your MVP—your mission, vision, and purpose—is in place. Of course, you need the right combination of factors. You have to be passionate about what you do. You need a spouse who really is a purpose partner, someone who supports your passion as much as you do and backs up that support with action. You have to want to be a mother as much as you want to be successful in business. And you must carve out time to get enough sleep and take care of yourself."

"Can you tell me a little more about the MVP?" Emily asked.

"My mission came out of my grief over losing my boyfriend, which happened when I was in my twenties," Simkins said. "I was trying to contemplate life and what I was supposed to do, and I would wake up every morning with swollen eyes from crying. Eventually, I knew I had to tell myself that I have a reason for being here, and I started to keep a journal. That journal became my lifeline.

"Every day I would say, 'I will live each day with purpose, divinely designed by God. I will walk with precision, I'll be guided by principle, I will receive prosperity and favor in every facet of my life. In this journey of life, it will be high, and it will be low, but there's one thing that I undeniably know: Goodness and mercy will follow me wherever I go. I hold fast to this promise, as I enjoy every moment of my life's journey.' And that became the mission statement that I would say to myself every single day to keep myself moving forward.

"I also had to have mission in front of mind once I started my business, because that needed a mission statement—a reason I was going out on my own. The MVP became a kind of mantra as I worked with the NFL, because I was trying to help players understand that their purpose included more than their performance on the field; their value was larger than the yardage they piled up. The MVP became the way to communicate that. So Mission–Vision–Purpose became the model for my work. But its genesis was me talking to myself to move myself back into life."

"Let's go back to the She-Suite for a minute," Emily said. "How did you decide to start an initiative focused on working women?"

"I wanted to bring to other women what I had been able to put together for myself," Simkins said. "Of course that meant I had to have it for myself before I could sell it to anyone else. I said to myself, *Well, if I'm going to put myself out there as an example, it won't be enough for me just to have a good life and a good job and make a good salary.* That kind of success challenges you to dream bigger, and I think that's what happened. I started to dream bigger, and not in terms of money or influence, but impact. I added a spouse to my vision of a wonderful life, and, in 2016, my adorable son, Kingston. I wanted to change people's lives, and I needed to change my life first, because I knew that if this could work for me, it could work for anyone else.

"Don't think for a minute that I didn't have help. Right at the beginning of establishing my own business, I ran into trouble. I had it worked out with my last corporate job that I would do consulting for them after I left, and that would give me a financial transition to being on my own. But at the last minute, they said, 'No, we can't do that. It has to be a clean break, with no consulting.' That was devastating, because that consulting work was my income for the first three months of my business.

"Soon after that, I was talking to a friend from high school, back in North Carolina, about my predicament, and he said, 'I got you. I'll cover your rent for the next three months. I knew in third grade that you're gonna do something big.' That generosity became the seeds from which my business grew. He didn't ask for anything, not even interest. How could I not share that with other people? That kind of generosity was in the DNA of my work.

"The hard part was creating Velvet Suite from scratch, with only me doing the actual work. It was kind of my own private leadership lab. I developed into a person who could stand before an audience and influence them. People would remark how confident and charismatic I was, and I'd tell them that it didn't come naturally, that becoming confident was a process that took me a long time to go through."

"That's difficult, changing yourself," Emily acknowledged.

"I was able to go through this process because I had faith and because while I wanted Velvet Suite to earn my living, I was more concerned with giving of myself and changing people's lives. My prayer life has been consistent, although now I have prayer partners who've helped me manifest my husband, my son, and my business. Whenever I've felt as if I'm not making progress, I've counted on prayer partners to talk me down, support me, laugh with me, encourage me. They've been very generous with *their* time."

"When you think of your role in moving women forward, how do you think about that responsibility? How do you think about your impact?" Emily asked. "I mean, you call it the She-Suite for a reason. How do you think about your responsibility to support and encourage other women, and not just in their business lives, but in their whole existence?"

"That's a fair question," Simkins replied. "It is a responsibility, and it can sometimes feel weighty. But I know it's not—it's God using me as an instrument. My responsibility is to stay close to God and to say, hey, it's bigger than I am. It's bigger than I thought it would ever be, and it's gonna get even bigger. But it's not *about* me, as long as I keep putting myself out of the way. If I tried to make this about me, it could be crushing, overwhelming. I'd have to hide my own inadequacies, and I have a lot of them; part of why I stay so close to this work is because it helps me get better.

"So I try not to make it about me. I try to give it to God to help me carry it, and God takes what's natural and makes it almost supernatural, in the way doors open for people who learn my process. I think of myself as a farmer, but one who just plants seeds. I'm always trying to do that. I feel that when you plant seeds, it just takes time, but they always come back full harvest. God makes the seeds grow and brings them to harvest, and my highest ambition is to live out my God-given purpose, and in my career, that purpose is to plant seeds of success.

> **"My highest ambition is to live out my God-given purpose, and in my career, that purpose is to plant seeds of success."**

"I believe that many people have the ability to shape culture and change people's lives. But they don't know they have it until they have a conversation about faith. When the door opened and the NFL became an opportunity, I don't think it was by accident. I think it was the Divine hand reaching out. With faith, what's been invisible becomes visible, and people recognize it. I try to reach some of these people. My personal relationship with God and my prayer communicate my vision, where I'm supposed to be, how I'm supposed to help, how I'm supposed to grow, what I'm supposed to learn behind the scenes."

"How are you generous with yourself?" Emily asked. "That is, how do you take care of yourself? What do you give to yourself?"

"Oh, that has not been easy," Simkins acknowledged. "I've had to recognize that with my personality type, the hardest thing for me to do is to rest. It's uncomfortable for me to choose self-care over work for others. Because Friday is the day that I typically don't schedule meetings, I'll often make appointments for things like hair and nails that day.

"Every quarter, I take time away and plan my next ninety days, and I sit with the gratitude of what happened during the previous ninety days. I pray and listen and just rest. I learned that practice from one of my mom's best friends, one of the first entrepreneurs whom I met personally. On Saturdays, she would lie in bed all day, explaining, 'That's how I get back to myself.' Following her example, I have a day for which I don't plan anything, and I make sure I take care of myself and rest.

"I also work out and drink lots of water. I keep a gallon jug of water in my office. Basically, I'd like to get old the way my parents have. They're so healthy and vibrant. I should have been paying more attention to how they were taking care of themselves when they were in their forties!"

"You're very committed to that ninety-day plan," Emily said. "Isn't that one of your premier speech topics?"

"That's right, Emily. I use it in many of my summits. The most recent had more than a thousand people."

"Wow," Emily said. "I'd call that generosity of scale, because you're not doing it just for you or for the money. You don't expect anything in return for your expertise. I can envision how that impacts people's lives and causes a ripple effect.

"Can you talk to me about branding?" Emily continued. "How is having a consistent brand part of personal growth, and how do you encourage people to build their brands?"

"Branding ties directly to generosity and faith," Simkins replied. "The brand was often used in early times when artists were making pots. They would put their thumbprint in it to mark it as a unique piece of art that had value because it was tied to that individual creator. So brand ties us to the way of creation and the Creator. He made each of us unique, as every fingerprint is unique.

"But a lot of people don't go to the Creator and ask, 'What is the operating manual for us as humans?' They can spend their whole lives doing things that don't match their purpose in life. It's the human equivalent of putting a smartphone in a microwave, which you know is inadvisable if you read the manual. But if you don't read your operator's manual and don't ask the Creator what His mark on you means, you may go through life oblivious of your reason for being. The Maker's mark is on us, and our journey to fulfilling that mark is the same as our quest for purpose. We're asking our Creator to help us unveil that purpose in a meaningful way, so that we can make an impact on the people's lives around us.

"I think one of my favorite verses is Romans 8:28: 'And we know that all things work together for good to those who love God, to those who are called according to His purpose.' Purpose has always been a key driver in my life from when I was a little girl, even when I didn't know it," Simkins said. "It's why I refer to my husband as my purpose partner; we pursue the same goals and work together to achieve them. And when you act with purpose, you can meet any challenge—the hard times, the unexpected tragedies. I kept reminding myself that everything is working together for my good. The challenges serve to shape a more deeply rooted faith."

These insights about purpose had Emily thinking about her own generation. "Many people my age and younger don't have adults in their lives who can show them how to read their operator's manual, so to speak, and pursue their quest for purpose, let alone how to be generous," she said. "They don't have mentors who will volunteer to guide or encourage them. How would you talk to someone young who doesn't have guideposts about the power of generosity?"

Simkins thought for a moment.

"I don't know that I have *the* answer, but I think it involves tapping into people's motivation," she said. "Young people do have motivation. Their job is to channel that motivation productively, to help them discover the *why* of what they do and to understand how generosity accelerates their journey once they can clarify what they want, where they see themselves going, and why they do what they do. Remember, generosity is like a seed: the plants that arise from it may be the guideposts. Or it may be like a boomerang that comes back to you when you least expect it, in response to something good you may have forgotten you did.

"I would also say, on a very basic, practical level, two things: generosity costs little or nothing, and it feels good, I mean inside you on the chemical level."

"Oh, yes," Emily said, smiling. "I've read a college course's worth of stuff on the hormones of generosity and how they affect your brain and body."

"Absolutely," Simkins said. "There's no greater joy that I feel as the joy I experience when I am able to help someone else or see the fruit of my helping someone else. I see a lot of young people today who are depressed and anxious. If they want to be happier, that's a good motivator to take up generosity as a practice or habit."

"One of the things I read this summer was a longitudinal study on happiness," Emily said. "The writers came to one conclusion: that the number one factor for building happiness in somebody's life is having deep, meaningful relationships with other people, which was no surprise. But the article went on to talk about how those relationships are based on trust and how trust gets built by people demonstrating authentic generosity. I had always thought trust derives from honesty and integrity. It never occurred to me that generosity played such a big role."

"Now you've come full circle, because you're talking about how generosity is tied to trust and to relationships," Simkins said. "I would just add that one of those relationships, ideally, is with God. I believe that all things are possible with God, and I'm living proof."

Emily wrapped up the interview shortly afterward and went to her rental car, parked in front of Simkins's house. After being in the air-conditioned office, Emily thought walking back outside would be like being hit with a hot, wet mattress. But the air seemed a little less oppressive now, and a breeze had come up. Still, it was summer in Virginia, and the AC in the car was a good implementation of self-care, she decided.

On her way out, Emily noticed that Simkins's neighborhood was full of the mature trees she'd been hoping to find, and she drove under the leafy canopy, thinking about Simkins's religiosity. Raised pretty much without God, Emily had no conception of God at all, not even the old-man-with-a-long-beard that had been so prevalent when she was a small child. The images of Jesus she had seen—gory and suffering when she went to her Catholic friends' First Communions, benevolent and soulful when Protestant friends were preparing for confirmation—had seemed silly. How did anyone know what Jesus looked like?

Couldn't you be generous without God in your life? Emily thought, easing into traffic. *Or am I missing something important? Good topic for my new journal.* Well, any survey of world religions would have to wait until this project was completed. She joined the parade of cars on Route 7, hoping some driver would be generous and let her into a through-lane. *After all, their generosity will come back to them,* Emily mused as she steered the wheel and looked out past her windshield into the sunny sky.

CHAPTER 15

RIDING HIGH: GLENN FROMMER

Emily gunned the rental car, a nondescript blue Camry, up I-70, wanting to make time in case she ran into traffic later. The plane had arrived in Denver at 11:00 a.m., and her appointment with Glenn Frommer wasn't till 4:00 p.m., but there'd been a wait getting the car. Although she had four hours to make a two-hour drive, Emily didn't want to take any chances.

When there was an opening between walls of rock, she marveled at the scenery. Emily thought the trees would be all evergreens and not show the change of seasons this crisp afternoon, but as she got closer to Vail, she saw flashes of yellow and gold starting to appear. In the distance, snow-topped mountains reminded her that she wasn't nearly as high above sea level as she could be—or felt.

Emily left the interstate at Vail Village and checked the route to Glenn Frommer's home office on her GPS after pulling over.

She figured he'd be halfway up a mountain, but Frommer lived not far from the village. She was early, so Emily drove around for a little while and stopped for coffee. It was too long before winter for skiing, but lots of hikers and bicyclists swarmed the village, and she noted long lines for gondola rides up the mountain. Reviewing what she'd read about Frommer, she noted that he'd been an executive in a number of companies related to his background as a chemical engineer, and he had sold two companies that he ran about ten years ago for enough money to set himself up as a venture capitalist. As a VC he had ownership in over one hundred companies and was definitely a mover and shaker, though way under the radar at this stage in his life.

Frommer's home and office were on a steep, curving wooded road, and his house was built into the hillside with beautiful views of Vail Mountain. He answered the door immediately and welcomed Emily into an enormous living room with a cathedral ceiling and a wide brick fireplace.

"You're right on time," Frommer said, smiling. "How was your trip?"

"The drive from Denver was beautiful," Emily said. "I wasn't expecting early foliage."

"You got here just in time to see the start of something beautiful."

Emily studied Frommer, thinking that he was more tanned and in way better shape than most older management types she had met. He was thin and athletic looking. And he wasn't wearing a suit; in fact, he looked as if he were about to strap on a backpack and climb one of the nearby mountains. He moved fluidly as he got Emily some water from the door of the fridge.

Frommer ushered Emily into his home office, which was as cluttered as the living room and kitchen were in perfect order. Reports, files, and loose papers were piled everywhere. Towers of paper stood on the big desk, every other piece of furniture, any shelf that had space, and even the floor. Emily was sure he knew where everything was that he needed, but the room still looked like a fire waiting to happen. Behind his desk was a wall full of family photographs, at least five generations' worth, and his desk seemed to bear every electronic device yet invented, sometimes more than one: computers, monitors, phones, external hard drives, iPads, and a host of chargers.

"Excuse me, I forgot to tidy up," Frommer said. He shoved over a couple of piles on a table so he could fit two more stacks from a sofa. Motioning for Emily to sit on the sofa, he snaked his desk chair around the desk and between two stacks of corporate reports to sit opposite Emily.

"I know, it looks like I'm a hoarder," Frommer said. "It wouldn't be so bad, but my wife won't let me bring papers into our bedroom or use another room for the overflow. This is how I work. Twenty years ago a boss of mine who saw my cluttered desk said, 'Hey, cluttered desk, cluttered mind,' and my response to him was, 'Hey, empty desk, empty mind.' I know there are people who are very good at not having a lot of papers on their desks, but that's not me. I have lots of balls in the air at any point in time, and my office shows it. These days it is very hard to focus on any one thing, so yeah, clutter."

"You have a lot of family photos."

"I sure do," Frommer said, twisting in his chair. "My grandparents are up there, some of their parents, and my mom and dad. They're the giants whose shoulders I stand on. And of course my wife and kids are there, all the important family times. I'm all about family. And over there is a bookshelf that has the books that have had a major impact on my life. I'm always grateful to people who turn me on to great books.

"My favorite is *Good to Great* by Jim Collins. It has been my bible in business. Collins reminds us to hire the right people, to keep more than one idea in your head at a time, be humble, don't be afraid to change, but stay focused. He's amazing. But there are many other books on the shelf that have kind of taught me interesting concepts or encouraged me to be the best version of myself, including the newest book by Michael Greger, *How Not to Die*. Still working on that one. But even if I haven't read one of those books in years, if I see it on the shelf, it reminds me of the good lessons I learned from it."

Emily nodded. "Nice collection. Well, Don told me you're an open book, so let's get started," she grinned. "Did you come from generous people?"

"I would say so," Frommer said, "though when I was younger, the generosity was pointed inward, toward the family. I grew up Jewish in Brooklyn and New Jersey, and when you grow up Jewish, you learn a lot about *tzedakah*, which in my family meant giving without expecting anything in return, being kind and charitable with no strings attached, just for the goodness of it. And you learn about looking to do a *mitzvah*, a good deed, every day."

"Based on your photos I assume you come from a big family?"

"Oh, yes," Frommer said smiling at the memory. "In my immediate family, just two sisters, but I had aunts, uncles, and cousins by the dozen. When we lived in Brooklyn, there were probably 150 relatives within five blocks in each direction."

"Whoa," Emily said. Her closest relatives were three states away when she was growing up.

"We moved out to central New Jersey when I was seven years old. My parents didn't have two nickels to rub together, but they bought a house so we could grow up in the suburbs. My grandfather owned a grocery store in Brooklyn with his brother Morris, and every Sunday we would take the one-hour drive from New Jersey to spend time with my extended family, including my grandparents.

"But before we drove back to New Jersey every week, my Grandpa Henry would have us at the store and 'sell' my parents groceries for the coming week. He would fill a big cardboard box with everything we needed, and my father would hand my grandfather a twenty-dollar bill to pay. But then my grandfather would go to the cash register, put in the twenty dollars, and give him thirty or forty dollars in 'change.' My grandfather was just that way, a very generous guy. He was an early example for me of how to be generous.

"The phrase 'family over everything' became the mantra for our family and still is. My daughter even had T-shirts made up. They have the word *Family*, then under that a solid line, and under that the word *Everything*." Frommer pointed to his chest, ran an imaginary line across it, then pointed under the line. "Get it? Family *over* Everything. It's a value that's still powerful a hundred years after my grandfather's birth. We talk about him and the impact he has had on our family to this day. Selfless giving was his way. He did it over and over. You help your family. You don't expect anything in return. It is a responsibility. You just do it. He was an incredible role model for us all.

"It's a responsibility. You just do it."

"But don't get me wrong," Frommer continued, "I recognize that where I am today is a direct result of generosity, not only my family's, but because mentors gave me their time and provided me with opportunities in my career, opportunities to learn and grow."

"In a way I'm learning that those people can be like extended family—caring for your well-being and potential," Emily said.

"Oh, sure. My family wanted me to be a doctor from the time I came out of the womb. They would actually call me Glenn the Doctor. I almost didn't have a choice, and often I wish I had gone to medical school like they wanted me to. But I graduated as a chemical engineer and worked in the chemical industry for twenty-five years. Along the way I earned an MBA in finance and qualified as a CPA.

"Over my career there probably were times I should have been fired because I screwed something up, but people were patient with me and let me kind of work through it. I didn't recognize that as generosity at the time either. But looking back I know that what kept me in business was good, mature, seasoned veterans who saw something in me that encouraged them to mentor me and give me those opportunities."

"You were lucky," Emily said, reflecting on her own initial conversation when Don called her into his office and the patience she now realized he had extended.

"I certainly was," Frommer replied. "I know that now, so these days, every year for the past nine years or so, I write five handwritten thank-you notes to let people know that I appreciate what they did for me. Many of them are people I haven't seen or spoken to in decades, like teachers from grade school and high school who made science and math sexy and fun and encouraged me to pursue passions. They taught me how to be a better person and to think more deeply. I write to family members who helped me, pointed me in the right direction. And to people who were senior to me in business and gave me great suggestions. A colleague in North Carolina whom I barely knew advised me to get my MBA. All I thought at the time was, *Well, this is a successful guy giving me advice, so I probably should pursue it.* He was smart, it was wise advice, and he took the time to care. Now I know that his advice allowed me to be where I am today."

I wonder if I've been grateful enough to Don, Emily thought.

"Could you have had that deeper perspective when you were younger?" she asked.

"I should have realized it wasn't just me," Frommer said. "I mean, I received all this generosity, and I don't think I did a good job of repaying it or paying it forward. I don't think I was a great boss who saw the same potential in younger people who worked for me. I didn't consciously help them enough to develop and create their own careers and their own successes. I guess I was more selfish. I saw greatness in people and put them in positions to be successful, but I think my primary objective was to have them help the company grow. I saw the success of my subordinates as important to my success as a leader, with the secondary objective of saying, 'Hey, this will be good for you too.'

"It wasn't until I sold the first business in 2013 that I thought, *Wow, there were so many people who were central to our success, I have to say 'Thank you.'* That's when I started writing letters. I wrote to the senior team of that business, saying thank you for being the key to its success. And whatever I can do to repay you, like being a reference or a mentor, helping you throughout your career, you can count on me. But even that was in response to their generosity instead of being proactive."

Frommer paused and Emily got the feeling there was something more he wanted to say. So she waited.

"Around that same time there were other life events that changed the way I thought about things, and how I did things," Frommer said with a soft smile. "I was diagnosed several years ago with poly-cystic kidney disease, PKD. In most cases, it's a genetically inherited, progressive disease where more and more cysts grow on your kidneys. The cysts are benign, but eventually they choke out kidney function, leading to kidney failure. When that happens, you have to go on dial-ysis, and ultimately you'll need a kidney transplant if you want to avoid death. Currently, it's untreatable and incurable. A lot of people have it and don't even know it until they have symptoms. Being diagnosed with PKD was an eye-opener for sure. My perspective on mortality and life changed significantly."

"How prevalent is PKD?" Emily asked with concern.

"It isn't what's called an *orphan disease*, where only a few hundred people a year develop it. About six hundred thousand people in the US have PKD and about twelve million around the world. But PKD is not very well publicized, and it's underfunded in terms of research.

"To that point, as someone who never believes there is *nothing* you can do, that there is always a solution to a problem, I couldn't take the diagnosis lying down. I wanted to get behind efforts that would help eradicate this disease. I got more involved in the PKD Foundation, got on their advocacy champions network and the research grant committee, which worked to allocate resources to research programs around the world. I joined the network that lobbied government representatives, asking them to support legislation to fight kidney disease. I started to see that if I truly gave all I had to this cause, I could help make a difference on several fronts, but mostly in people's lives.

> **"I started to see that if I truly gave all I had to this cause, I could help make a difference."**

"During this time, a friend recommended that I sit down with a life planner. I had done a lot of strategic planning for my businesses, but I had never been in therapy and never focused inwardly on who I am and what I want to do for the remainder of my life. Come to think of it, Don also once asked me who I wanted to be. And I didn't have a great answer."

"Did the life planner help?" Emily asked.

"Oh, yes," Frommer said. "I sat with a great coach named Erik Jacobson for two very impactful days. The first day was about who I am, how I got to be who I was, and the second day was about who I wanted to be for the rest of my life. It forced me to look back at personal and professional decisions, actions, and think deeply about what was important and why. Erik asked great questions: How do you want to use your strengths and your gratitude? How do you want to build your life going forward? We developed a life plan with lots of elements to it, and the biggest element was about giving back and how I could build that into my life. That includes self-generosity; for the first time I thought about what really drives me, what makes me joyful. Talking to Erik set a course-corrected path that I never would have imagined before. It was so powerful, and I was so moved by the experience that I helped four others go through the same process! It was my first act of generosity using my new priorities and the new way of thinking. But the most visible result of the process with Erik was the RideForPKD."

"I've heard about this epic ride; please, tell me more."

"I rode my bike across America," Frommer said simply. "Beth, my wife, and I spent twenty weeks on the road. She was really the MVP of the ride: She drove a thirty-five-foot RV towing a Jeep Cherokee with six bikes on top and in the back of it—and she doesn't even like to drive. She handled all the logistics, too, and my sister Amy handled public outreach to let people know what we were up to. All I had to do was ride my bike, and I'd been a serious cyclist for thirty-five years. The goal was to raise five hundred thousand dollars for the PKD Foundation and raise awareness of the disease across the United States."

"So your ride was about three thousand miles?"

"More like fifty-five hundred! We started in San Francisco on May 1, 2022, and finished in Cape Cod on September 3. We had a circuitous route because we met with researchers at universities and with state legislators to give updates on the foundation's research and advocate for our legislative priorities. I also met a lot of PKD patients along the way. I met families who lost infants to PKD at thirty-seven days of age, teenagers who are already on dialysis, young adults in their twenties and thirties who have already had multiple kidney transplants, patients in their forties and fifties struggling to hold on to any kidney function, and others in their sixties and seventies who suffered from several of PKD's devastating effects. It was so inspiring to show up and see how excited these people were for us and our ride. It took a lot of time, but showing up for them was worth it.

"We were also able to encourage sufferers to engage in clinical trials and the PKD Registry, to help researchers help our community," Frommer said. "It got really emotional toward the end of the ride, when a lot of old friends and relatives rode with me to the finish line in Cape Cod, Massachusetts. Celebrating with loved ones was an incredibly special moment that I will forever be grateful for."

"Sounds like a successful trip."

"It was. We were covered by dozens of TV and print and other media outlets, and we raised $654,000, exceeding our fundraising goal. Seven or eight members of Congress and state legislators met with us, and we also had meetings with chapters of the PKD Foundation. Mind you, I had no idea what the hell I was doing. I had never done anything like this before, but I felt like I was doing good and maybe making up for lost time.

"Even better than the exposure, we touched the lives of hundreds of PKD sufferers and their families, often sharing best practices and providing introductions or contacts for people who otherwise would have been sitting on the couch waiting to get sicker. The trip also had a big impact on me and Beth. The incredible inspiration and motivation in this effort and the energy we derived from it were orders of magnitude beyond what I expected. As we completed the journey, Beth asked me, 'What are we going to do next?' And that was the perfect question. That's how we're living our lives."

"What a great story, your personal journey and the ride. But if you don't mind me asking, what effect has this had on your family given how close you are?" Emily asked.

"Great question. I have three grown children: Matt, Rachel, and Jake. Two of them live in Denver and one in Boulder. We all love to be out in nature, skiing, hiking, biking, so it's great to have them here in Colorado. And they're old enough and smart enough to understand what a transformation I was going through.

"About three years ago, I sat down with Beth and the kids and said, listen, we have an opportunity to make a difference in the lives of others, but I know we all have different passions and concerns. So let's do some research and find organizations that carry out work you think is important *and* are also well run."

With a grin he added, "Just because I'm leading with my heart doesn't mean my business brain isn't also at work. So, we agreed by the end of that family meeting that each of us would choose five charities, all five of us would review the twenty-five, and then we would allocate what we could in the ways we could to those organizations.

"And we took that task very seriously. In addition to learning what we could online, we actually called each charity to discuss things like the mission, community engagement, impact, and how donations were used. And then we gave and, in some cases, became involved."

"Was that the first time you'd engaged with nonprofits?"

"Oh, no. When I first worked in the chemical industry, I worked for a company that expected all its employees to give 5 percent of their salaries annually to a specific organization. It was similar to the way we gave *tzedakah* growing up. I gave happily. But after a while I kind of soured on the huge nonprofit idea. When you donate to it, you're not quite sure where your money is going and how decisions are made. It's a black hole. And more than that, when it's money that comes from your check, there's not an emotional attachment. I want my kids to think sincerely and proactively about charity work. And that takes a deeper level of commitment than an annual donation.

"Look, I understand having made money it could be easy for my kids to think fancy things are what money is about. But Beth and I want to emphasize for them that material things don't bring lasting joy. They don't solve real-world problems. We want our lives to be more focused on helping those who perhaps can't help themselves. That is part of *our* mission statement as a family. That's what my parents and grandparents taught me. And it's really been driven home for me this past decade."

"But if your kids are around my age, do you ever worry you're kind of late with your messaging?" Emily asked, silently feeling a small doubt creep in about whether she could make the big changes she had been so excited about.

"Oh, they got the memo without any help from me," Frommer said. "Matt was an architect, but he went back to school and got a master's in environmental studies. Now he works for a nonprofit. He used to work in transportation, and now he's involved in housing issues. Everything he does is focused on doing what's right for the environment and broader community. Rachel is an outstanding pediatric nurse because, she says, she is driven by and has a passion for taking care of people. My youngest, Jake, is in the live music business. He knows the joy that music brings to people. If anyone's responsible for how they turned out, it's my wife, Beth. She's a very giving, generous person.

"When I was a kid, the message was, do all the good that you can, but be financially successful. That's one of the reasons my family wanted me to be a doctor, because I could help others *and* make a nice living. It's different now. Of course we want our kids to be financially stable, but more than that, I want them to pursue their passions. If they can make a living doing it, great. I now appreciate how much of their growing up was about encouraging them to invest in themselves so they could become the best versions of themselves and then give back to the community."

"It does sound as if your kids got that message."

"Matt and his wife, who is an epidemiologist working for the state of Colorado, know they could double their salaries tomorrow if they went into private enterprise, but they tell us they wouldn't feel good about it because they'd be beholden to the company rather than doing what is right and what's good for people. Rachel helps sick kids and their families navigate difficult health challenges, and it's incredibly taxing work both physically and emotionally. Jake is really drawn to the joy that music brings to an audience. They all work to support broader communities and make a positive difference in the world. By contrast, I was in the chemical and packaging industries, and my products and services never brought joy to people in the same way. They filled a need, but no one thinks about what glue does or what packaging does. I'm really proud of all my kids' choices."

"Thank you," Emily said, feeling a little relief that it wasn't too late for her.

"I know you have to run soon, but can I share something I'm really excited about, speaking of work to be proud of?" Frommer asked.

Emily nodded eagerly.

"For the past several years, I've been running a venture capital investing group called Milkbox Partners with one of my cousins. We specialize in problem-solvers over a wide variety of areas, some tech-related, some in real estate, some environmental, more than a hundred investments in all."

"Why Milkbox?" Emily asked.

"Glad you asked. It's a shout-out to my grandfather. Before he had refrigeration, he had this "milk box" outside his grocery store in Brooklyn, a big, insulated wooden box with ice all around it, where he'd put all the things that would spoil, like cheese, milk, and eggs. That milk box was a central gathering point for our entire family on weekends and holidays. We'd say, 'Hey, see you at the milk box at two.' Thanksgiving, Rosh Hashanah, any holiday we were in Brooklyn, we were always meeting at the milk box. And because my grandfather had such an impact on our lives, we decided to name our investing partnership in his honor. He was my cousin's grandfather too."

"That's pretty generous, setting up venture capital."

"Hear me out. You might be able to argue that the most powerful form of generosity is helping other people be successful. And that's what we're doing. We're giving people with passion and purpose, and a plan, a chance to live out their dreams and create those opportunities. I know it's not exactly the same as serving at a soup kitchen, volunteering at a food pantry, or helping build a house with Habitat for Humanity. But it's a form of generosity that gets at the core of helping someone else succeed for no other reason than to help them succeed.

> **"We're giving people with passion and purpose, and a plan, a chance to live out their dreams and create those opportunities."**

"Speaking of Habitat for Humanity, we used to bring our kids to work weekends for the organization. We never asked them to analyze the experience though, like *how did you feel about doing that?* But we always made sure they met people who were going to be living in the houses, saw their joy. I really think that helped them realize the value that comes from being generous with your time and making other people happy."

"Too bad all kids don't have parents like you," Emily said sincerely. "A lot of the twenty- and thirtysomethings I know are all about money so they can pay off their student loans or take a vacation from work."

"I think most middle-class parents are still raising their children about the same way my parents raised me: get a good education, make money, get married, take care of your family," Frommer said. "So your generation doesn't know how to be generous any more than mine did unless you're told how, shown how, and given chances to do it."

"It probably doesn't help that my generation is apparently more inwardly focused than outwardly," Emily said.

"Sure, that may have something to do with it," Frommer said. "In any case, I think it's super-important to help people move forward on the journey toward generosity, whether that help comes early or late. It may be as much about age as anything else. I certainly never thought of myself as particularly generous or giving until perhaps the last ten years. I always *appreciated* generous people, but I didn't really understand *how* to be generous until my hair got a lot grayer and sparser. No one explicitly talked to me about generosity and the power of giving, but everyone was very explicit about how to be successful in business. I think a lot of people want to be generous, but they don't know how."

"Does that include being generous to yourself?"

"I think so. I have become more generous with my own health. The kidney thing aside, I want to be around for as long as possible in a healthy way. I've got a new granddaughter, and I want to see her grow up and have all those great milestones in her life. So I have tried to become more generous with my own health and focus on it.

"My own dad didn't do that. He died at sixty-two. Because he wasn't self-generous. His generosity was all about the family. He was so good to my mom and me and my two sisters. As a CPA, he probably did about two hundred tax returns a year, and sixty of those were for family members and friends, whom he never charged a dime.

"And he did all that to the detriment of his own health. He never took care of himself. He never invested in himself, so from the age of probably forty-eight until he died, he had one health ailment after another that could have been controlled. He ignored them at his own peril and a huge loss for the family. He missed twenty years he could have had with his family. I want to avoid that. That's why I have kind of been a fitness junkie and eat healthy. I try to do the right things for myself because I think if I can take care of myself, it gives me that longevity to take care of others."

"You've given me a lot to think about," Emily said. "Is there anything else you want to tell me?"

Frommer shook his head. "I really laid out my life for you," he said. "I never realized before how much I'm a work in progress."

"But that's good," Emily said. "That's a youthful way of thinking."

"True," Frommer said. "Still too young to have the wisdom of the sages. Hopefully I will get there one day and still be healthy enough to share it."

"I hope so," Emily said.

Frommer showed Emily to the front door and wished her success with her personal journey. Emily walked out into a lovely twilight under the evergreens. Getting into her car, she wondered if any of the stores in Vail were still open so she could buy a pair of hiking boots. Pinafore was putting her up in the village overnight, and her plane didn't leave Denver till evening. *A hike through the aspens, watching the yellow leaves drop down, might be just the thing,* Emily thought, taking out her phone. *But first, I'm gonna call Mom.*

CHAPTER 16

I BELIEVE IN YOU:
ANDRE DURAND

Still half-asleep, Emily followed the crowd to the A line at Denver International, holding tight to her silver rolling bag with one hand and her briefcase with the other. The call hadn't come until 8:00 p.m. the previous night: Andre Durand, CEO of Ping Identity had agreed to squeeze her in at eleven the next morning—could Emily catch a 5:00 a.m. flight from San Diego to Denver? Durand was leaving for Asia later in the week, and no one knew when he'd be Stateside again. "Of course, sure, no problem," Emily said, already packing with one hand as she held her phone in the other.

She'd been sort of awake in the Uber to SDI at 4:00 a.m., but she was sound asleep (in business class, thank goodness) when the plane took off and throughout the two-hour flight. Now, less than twelve hours since getting that phone call, she was marching through the Denver airport again, desperate for coffee but unwilling to stand in a long Starbucks line until she was actually downtown and knew she could make her appointment on time, given the hour time difference.

Emily was lucky enough to get on a train that was about to leave and was delivered to Union Station in the promised thirty-seven minutes. When the oasis—the coffee place, that is—appeared just twenty paces toward the street, it was only 9:30 Mountain Daylight Time. She could sit for at least forty-five minutes and sip a nice big Americano while she learned something about Durand.

Andre Durand, an alumnus of UC Santa Barbara, had been developing software for thirty years, establishing, building, and selling one successful enterprise after another. He entered the Internet security industry when he co-founded Ping Identity in 2002. With round after round of funding, Ping grew until it had offices worldwide and went through a successful IPO. By the time private equity firm Thoma Bravo bought the company for $2.8 billion in 2022, Ping had fourteen hundred employees, and Durand was an *eminence gris* in identity protection. He was heralded by many publications as an energetic technology visionary.

> **"Is there anything more generous**
> **than believing in someone?"**

Once she was properly fueled by caffeine, Emily noted that the Ping building was just a few blocks away, too close for an Uber. She picked up her rolling bag and briefcase, and walked down a street of glass, steel, and concrete, dotted with bistros and boutiques, that could have been any street in any American big-city downtown. But just before Emily turned the corner toward her destination, a park opened before her, and she was charmed enough by the dogs running and playing in the off-leash area to stand and watch for a few minutes.

Emily walked into the gleaming glass building that housed Ping Identity and rode up a long, two-floor escalator as instructed. At the top, she saw something she had never seen in an upscale office tower before: a brand-new, full-service two-story gym, easily thirty thousand square feet, that included a free-weight area, every possible workout machine, and a four-lane lap pool, with what looked like a cold plunge and a larger heated pool in the distance. A running track, halfway between floor and ceiling, encircled the gym. The whole thing must have taken up most of that side of the building, if not the entire side.

At almost 11:00 a.m., only a few people were present. Emily, trained to calculate space, began to count up how many people could work in that area: a lot. *This company must have one heck of a break room*, she thought.

Emily crossed the floor to the Ping reception desk, where a young woman greeted her warmly and said Mr. Durand's assistant, Dana, would be right down. In a moment, Dana appeared and took Emily up to Durand's office, a large but comfortable den of tan leather and off-white linen, with two glass walls. Durand, a boyish, athletic man in his fifties, came out from behind a large red oak desk with a big smile and a hand extended in greeting. For someone who had just agreed to squeeze Emily into a tight schedule, Durand seemed unruffled and unhurried.

"Hello, Emily," Durand said. "May I call you Emily? I'm Andre."

"Of course," Emily replied cheerfully. "Thank you so much for making the time to see me. I understand you're going abroad soon. That must take a lot of preparation."

"Not usually, but this time I'm taking the family," he said. "But that isn't the reason you were summoned at the last minute. Dana is very protective of my time, and your visit didn't jump to the top of her list until I got a call from Don."

"Aha," Emily said. Don's demeanor was relaxed, but he would not be denied.

"He reminded me that I'd promised to give you an interview, and he knew I was going away in a few days. I agreed, and now you're here."

"And I'm very happy to be here," Emily said. "How much do you know about what I'm now calling Pinafore's generosity project?"

"Pretty much what Don has told me," Durand replied. "Pinafore is further aligning itself with the focus of generosity, and it's sent you to interview people who are known for understanding its importance. Don knows I fall into that category."

"Indeed," Emily said, admiring his subtle confidence. "I would like to focus on how you've helped other people to be successful and how your generosity toward others was nurtured. The floor is yours."

Durand looked thoughtful for a moment.

"I've definitely benefited from other people's generosity, both generosity of belief and generosity of trust," he said. "That happens when people believe in our dreams and trust us to carry them out.

"We all have hopes and dreams, especially when we're young. We want to create a good life for ourselves: find a job, make enough money to support ourselves, maybe support a family. We ask ourselves, *Can I make it? Am I good enough? What am I going to do? Who can help me?* Our words have no weight, and we have little reputation. But we're filled with hope. And in those transformative years, if we're lucky, some people come along and listen to us and believe in us. It's a generosity that doesn't cost much, but it means everything."

Durand sighed.

"I'm seeing this in my own daughters right now, as they begin the mental journey of separation from the nest, the backpack of anxiety on their shoulders. How successful are they going to be? How are their mother and I going to feel about them, given how high the bar has been raised, at least in their perception? All they know is the lifestyle that Kim and I have created. And can they top that? Do they need to do better than I did? Do they even need our help?"

"I would think they'd be confident about the future," Emily said.

She wondered, *Would having a very successful father like Andre be an advantage or a detriment?* She could see it going either way.

"Maybe," Durand replied, "but they may want to be in totally different fields and not sure how to get there. They may be looking at a time when their efforts won't buy them the lifestyle they grew up with—they know Kim and I will help, but they may not want our help and we sure won't subsidize a lot of luxury and indulgence."

"Mm-hmm," Emily said. "Looking back, who was your first mentor?"

"He was this guy I knew when I was in high school, I guess a rich guy, and I helped him build a kit car. All the parts came in this huge box, and you had to assemble it into an actual car that you could drive. He wasn't prepared to do that himself, so I worked on it after school every day. I had this idea for a company, and one day I told him. He said, 'Hold on a second,' and he left the room. He came back with a check made out to me for ten thousand dollars. That was a lot of money for me. I grew up in a poor family with very modest means.

"He never thought he was making an investment. It was generosity; he figured he'd never see that money again. But he was showing his belief in me. That scene has been repeated three or four times during my career, when somebody much older or wiser or more successful backed something I was doing in business, without any expectation of return or success. They believed."

"That's amazing," Emily said.

"It is! You never know when you're going to meet someone who believes in you. It's like that movie *Sliding Doors*, where the second of catching or not catching the train determines your fate. I met the guy who bought my first company by chance. We chatted at a conference for maybe five or ten minutes, but he remembered me, and later he acquired my first company, plus he moved me to Denver, and I married his assistant. I launched my second company out of the company he continued to build.

"The sequence of events that led me here undeniably took a fork in the road at the moment in which this man believed enough to acquire my first company," Durand continued. "And I don't think he saw something in the company or the tech. I think he saw something in me, and he took a chance and bestowed a certain amount of belief and trust in me, and that made all the difference. Is there anything more generous than believing in someone? I'm not sure."

"That was a lucky meeting," Emily said.

"It certainly was, though I don't know that I believe in luck *per se*," Durand said. "Good fortune usually builds on some foundation you have created. When someone has had a string of successes, it's easy to believe that their next act will be a success. You don't have to trust. But when there's no track record of success, it takes a tremendous amount of trust to think that someone's venture is going to work out. Go back to the early parts of anyone's career. You're hungry for anyone to see you or to believe in you. It takes small acts of belief and trust early to have a significant impact on the trajectory of someone's life. It also takes small acts by the would-be recipient to gain the attention of the giver. Though I was interested in building that car, I knew I was being generous helping him out. I didn't dream that it would lead where it did."

> "It takes small acts of belief and trust early to have a significant impact on the trajectory of someone's life."

Emily nodded, realizing that Don had believed in her when she was still in college. *I'm so fortunate to have had him in my life,* she thought. *Have I been taking him for granted all these years?*

"Anyway, it's best when it happens during youth," Durand said. "If you change the trajectory of someone's life by a degree when they're five years old, they could end up on the other side of the world. When you're seventy, being moved one degree isn't going to affect your life much, but one degree when you're young will have significant impact. That make sense?"

"Yes, it does. So, how do you define generosity?" Emily asked. "Is it a willingness to believe in someone and trust someone enough to give them money, or is it more than that?"

"To start with, there are degrees of generosity, maybe degrees of *purity* of generosity," Durand said. "For example, who's more generous, the person who has only a dime but gives away that dime to someone who needs it more, or the person with hundreds of millions of dollars who gives away a million? Both can have a positive impact on people's lives."

"True," Emily said. The example of someone giving away his only dime stirred something in her memory, but she couldn't put her finger on it yet.

"If I have to define generosity, I guess it means believing in someone when there is no reason to believe, followed by trust where there is no reason to trust," Durand said. "I've always thought that the purest form of generosity has no expectation of a desired outcome. You aren't generous to become more successful, though ultimately it works that way. For me, that's made all the difference.

"There might *be* a financial return, of course, and there's often a return on generosity in the happiness it brings you. But true generosity has no expectancy of return from the individual or individuals you are giving to. It's just the right thing to do, and when you do experience gain from it, it's almost a responsibility to pay it forward."

"How does that translate to the culture of your company?" Emily asked.

"Well, this is going to sound preachy, but whatever," Durand said. "Generosity in the workplace means putting human beings ahead of profit. You'll hear C-suite types talk about 'hitting the numbers by any means possible.' You can sacrifice a lot of humans in the pursuit of profit. Our philosophy is that it doesn't work to achieve the profit and sacrifice the culture. In line with what generosity is, we want everyone in our company to succeed."

"That makes sense," Emily agreed.

"In an ungenerous corporate culture, you're new to the company. You don't know anyone or anything, so you ask someone for help. Let's say the person you ask is a more senior person in another department, but they happen to be seated next to you. If that person says, 'Who are you, and whom do you report to?' or 'I'm busy, go ask your manager,' you don't have a healthy culture.

"If that person stops what they're doing and says, 'Oh, you're new! Let me show you. Let me tell you where you need to go and what you need to do and whom you need to talk to. You know what, I'll walk you over there and introduce you...' *That's* a healthy culture. People do this without an agenda. It's who they are and who the company is. Everyone wants you to be successful.

"It doesn't take much encouragement to get most people into a zone where helping is natural. It means putting the team ahead of your own contribution, collaboration over competitiveness—and competitiveness comes naturally to a lot of people. And a collaborative culture has to come from the top, because what I described can have costs in terms of productivity. But I really believe that a healthy culture will be the winner in the long term. Didn't Peter Drucker say, 'Culture eats strategy for breakfast'?

"Anyway, I consider myself a servant leader. This isn't new thinking, but many more are recognizing the power in this style of leadership," Durand said. "Long-term thinking is important. Of course, companies want to retain customers, but their leaders should understand that to retain customers, most companies must retain their key talent. Those are the firms that build more value. A culture of generosity, where both employees and customers feel sincerely valued, promotes trust, and business thrives on trust. I can't stress this enough."

Emily smiled and nodded. Durand was obviously very passionate and she was really beginning to feel the same passion. Almost every interview had reflected on this to some extent.

"I think that you shouldn't judge a person or a circumstance by a photograph, which captures only a moment in time," Durand continued. "Judge us by the movie of our lives, which isn't over until we're gone. Every scene plays an important role in what happens next and how the movie ends. Judge us by who we become.

"As I think about my life, there's some sense of urgency, because I don't know how long I'm going to live. If I have a hundred years from this moment to give back, chances are I'll be able to give back more than I've received. But what if I have only five years? When I'm on my deathbed, I don't want to look back and regret anything I did or how I did it.

"So, getting back to corporate culture, I would have deep regrets if I didn't care about my employees' well-being and health. If I asked fathers or mothers to work extraordinary hours and ultimately sacrifice time with their kids, I'd be contributing to the break-up of families, which has a multigenerational cost to society. I'd be externalizing the cost of my profit to society in the form of broken families. That's unacceptable."

"Did you have a generous parental role model when you were growing up?" Emily asked.

"Oh, sure, my mother," Durand said. "And my grandmother, who lived with us till I was about sixteen. Their mantras were 'Work hard, be kind, do good, do the right thing.' My mother had lots of opportunities to do good things, and she'd tell me about them. Not bragging, just showing me that there were a lot of ways to make the world a better place."

"How do you impart that kind of thinking to people who weren't raised with role models like you had?" Emily asked. "Especially younger people, since at some point we *will* be in charge."

"I don't know the answer," Durand replied. "Technology has made the world much smaller, and people under thirty have grown up steeped in it. They're even more aware of our interconnectedness than people who are older. They're aware of issues that affect them now and will affect them the rest of their lives, like the cost of living and climate change. That's actually healthy, I think. It's easy to be oblivious and naive, but quite another to have been exposed to suffering that you didn't know was there. I'd like to think that humans become more empathetic when technology allows them to see the entire world as it is."

"But technology has also given political voices a lot of platforms," Emily said. "And what we see via technology is manipulated so easily that often, it's hard to tell what's real or fake."

"That's very true," Durand said. "People grab the mic and never give it back. Everyone in the middle is silent, and everyone on the edges is screaming, and to many people, the world seems to be black-and-white when, in fact, it's every possible shade of gray. And those shades of gray are where most of the world lives."

He paused for a moment.

"Come to think of it, those shades of gray include people of every age, not just young people," Durand said. "I think it's fine to begin to explore the generosity journey at any point in a person's life. Those seeds can germinate at any time."

"So you believe that if you're authentically generous, with no expectation of return, the indirect benefits to you will be significant throughout your life?" Emily asked.

"I do believe that, a hundred percent," Durand said.

"But bad behavior seems to be rewarded too," Emily said. "I haven't turned thirty yet, and I've seen bad behavior rewarded at times."

"I've seen it too; we call it succeeding from failure to failure," Durand said.

Emily laughed. She liked that phrase—succeeding from failure to failure. That was one to remember, she decided.

"But technology is catching up there too," Durand was saying. "It's locating poor behavior faster and faster. It used to be that you could run from your actions by moving to another city, but technology has collapsed geography enough so that the employer in Seattle knows the work history of the prospective employee from Cleveland. If I behave poorly at one company, then try to get a job at the second, the employer at the second company is going to be able to connect the dots in a way that they couldn't twenty years ago. And remember, we're talking about human beings here. You never know when a charmer is going to meet an employer who's susceptible to charm or when a supervisor who doesn't care about personalities hires someone who's toxic but has the skills.

"Obviously, you have to be careful and responsible as an employer, but if you're good at what you do and you're a decent judge of people, you'll make good decisions," Durand said. "These days a lot of employers, when a staffer leaves, won't give any opinion, bad or good, in a recommendation letter. They'll just say 'Yeah, this individual worked at this company from this date to that date.'

"But the savvy boss will pick up the phone and ask, 'Okay, what do you really think?' The former employer who wants to give a stellar recommendation, if they haven't already, will say, 'Yes, this person is great, has done amazing things, I'm sorry to lose them, you should hire them immediately.' But if the prospective employee underperformed or has a toxic personality, the former supervisor will probably stick to the work dates. One of the things my mother taught me was 'If you can't say anything nice, don't say anything at all.'

"Good employers look at the person sitting across from them and recognize that what they're looking at is just a snapshot. They then try to put together the movie of the person's life before and after that meeting. What they've done, what they didn't have the option to do, what they might do in the future. Karma is whether that consideration opens or closes the door in front of someone. Today, and into the future, bad karma will follow you faster, and so will good karma. I guess you could say that technology will be a karma accelerator. A reputation of generosity will be more important than ever."

> **"Today, and into the future, a reputation of generosity will be more important than ever."**

"Is there science to any of this?" Emily asked, rapt. "You know, to becoming a generous person, or identifying one, or channeling someone's latent generosity?"

"Everything has a science. The key is to discover it," Durand said. "There's a formula, and it sounds like Don's asking you to figure out what that formula is."

"I'm glad they didn't give me something hard to do," Emily said, and they both laughed.

"Then again, maybe there are many formulas," Durand said, returning to his theme. "For some people, generosity comes naturally, as it did to me, and I was also blessed with a personality that made people believe in me and trust me—that is, want to be generous to me. Maybe they saw generosity inherent in me. I can't take credit for that, nor for my circumstances: born in the United States, to certain parents at a certain time and place, circumstances that allowed me to approach the world with a certain risk tolerance. Luck of the draw.

"But not everyone is me. For some people, the propensity for generosity is latent, pushed down by upbringing or training that preaches 'Every man for himself' or that the bottom line is sacred. You might have to reach a person trained that way with magazine articles and longitudinal studies. In the end, I think they will need to see generosity in action. When you see the power of generosity in action, it's difficult to deny.

"You might touch someone's hidden moral compass by demonstrating your way is ethically correct and expressing it in a way that speaks to the individual. You might not be able to convince someone that action with no expectation of return is optimal, but you might get the next best thing if you explain that being generous has excellent returns and will make that person happy. More important, you will need to model generosity."

Emily sighed inwardly with relief. *I can live with that.*

"Everyone starts in a different place," Durand continued. "I don't know if there's one universal hook. There may be one formula for generosity, but there may be a dozen ways to connect to that formula and apply it to attain happiness and success. If you figure out that algorithm, please let me know. It's really a fascinating thing to ponder."

"Last topic," Emily said, lost in the ideas Durand was sharing with her. "How are you generous with yourself? In other words, how do you take care of yourself so you can keep being generous to others?" Emily had grown very comfortable with the balance between generosity with others and self-generosity. She loved learning everyone's preferred methods and marveled at how different the formulas were for each person.

Durand thought for a while before he spoke.

"Sometimes self-care seems self-indulgent," he began, his voice increasingly firm. "But I keep telling myself that the empty cup has little to give; if you rob yourself of what it means to both be healthy and happy, you aren't in much of a position to give.

"I think of it in terms of sustainability. If you want to maximize your ability to give over the long term, you can't ignore your well-being. If you give at the cost of your health, you're going to give for a short period of time. If you want to give for a hundred years, you'd better take care of yourself.

"I think of my physical health and energy as a battery. We're all born with a certain size battery, some bigger than others. Your battery charges at a certain speed, discharges at a certain speed, and recharges while we sleep. The battery loses 10 percent of its capacity each decade after age twenty, so at twenty the battery is charged to 100 percent, but when we're sixty, it charges to just 60 percent, and it takes more hours of recharging to get to 60 percent when we're older than it took to charge to 100 percent when we were twenty.

"At a certain age, stress and anxiety drain your battery faster than when you were young, and so do activities to which you didn't give a thought in your twenties. For example, if I go out drinking tonight, that's going to have a big impact on my energy the next day. I have to decide whether drinking tonight is worth devoting most of tomorrow to recharging."

Emily nodded in agreement.

"I've become pretty good at managing stress brought on by workload, but I'm not as good as I want to be in terms of exercise," Durand added. "I need to get on that, and watching what I eat, because there are days that I need every bit of battery power I have. I even color-code my calendar so I can predict what I'll need in terms of energy. 'Vision sessions,' when I'm in front of customers, and have to be my best, are marked in purple, and board meetings are red. If I see a day on my calendar that's all purple and red, I know that day is going to take a lot of energy."

Brilliant, she thought. *Tracking the energy you will need to expend by hour, by day. Someone should create an app for that.*

"You look as if you could bear up," Emily said, with the slightest bit of outward admiration.

"I've been very, very lucky," Durand said.

"Any final thoughts? I know you have a lot to do," Emily said.

"What can I say?" Durand said, shrugging. "I've been successful. I had help, and I've helped others. Being of service and being kind is a pretty sure road map to happiness and success. I might also suggest you play around a bit with AI (artificial intelligence), if you haven't already. ChatGPT was one of the original platforms and is pretty good. Pose some questions about generosity into an AI of your choice and see what you get. You'll likely learn something new about the power of generosity but also get a taste of where the world is rapidly headed. My prediction is that generosity will play an even bigger role in success as time passes.

Emily thanked Durand. He rose and smiled, they shook hands, and she left his light-filled office. With the interview concluded, the before-dawn rising caught up with her, and she yawned as she rode the escalator to the first floor. *I have some work to do*, she thought. She knew about ChatGPT but hadn't tried using it. Perhaps AI could help her come up with next steps, a way to share knowledge, this one simple thing, with the world.

She smiled to herself. Yep, she was sold. This is something she really wanted to do. How the heck did Don know she was the one? Why did he believe in her? Durand's comment about believing in someone as the ultimate form of generosity was front and center in her mind. If being grateful was being generous, she was feeling very generous.

Pinafore, very graciously, did not require Emily to return to San Diego the same day, and she headed for Denver's downtown Pinafore Hotel, which was right around the corner. On the way, the source of someone giving away his only dime struck her. It was a classic book she'd read as a child, *A Little Princess*. A girl at a posh boarding school in London finds out that her wealthy father has been ruined financially, and the headmistress puts her to work as a scullery maid. One day, the girl is walking down the street and finds a sixpence coin on the pavement. She goes into a bakery and buys six buns for a treat. Outside the bakery, the girl sees a ragged, homeless girl and gives her one of her buns, which the other girl wolfs down. The heroine puts down bun after bun until she's given the ragged girl five of the six, then walks off munching the last one.

I wonder if I could have done that, Emily pondered. *Definitely more likely now than six months ago.* She yawned again, grateful to see the Pinafore's welcoming entryway and eager to get situated in her room. Like so many of the Pinafore properties she'd overseen, the staff was gracious, kind, and efficient in checking her in and sending her up to her room.

CHAPTER 17

EMILY'S EPIPHANIES

The phone rang three times. Emily didn't really expect Don to answer, but he did, and he did so enthusiastically.

"Well, hello Emily, I figured I might hear from you soon. I understand you are finished with your interviews," Don said.

"Are you checking up on me?" Emily said, half kidding.

"Not exactly," Don replied. "I have received a lot of nice messages from the people you have met with. You made very positive impressions. I'm not surprised. So, are you really finished?"

"Well," Emily said, "I do have one more to do."

"Oh. Who remains?" Don asked.

"I've left the best for last," Emily said. "I would like to interview you!"

There was a pause on the line. She could almost see Don smiling.

"I love that," he replied. "Absolutely. I'm in Texas at our West Legacy Pinafore this week. It's in Plano just north of Dallas, only

243

about twenty minutes from DFW. Let me know when you'll be here and I'll schedule a conference room."

"Perfect," Emily replied. "Can't wait to see you again. We have a lot to catch up on."

They both said their goodbyes and hung up.

Emily smiled to herself thinking about the past few months. At last, she fully comprehended the incredible gift and opportunity Don had given her. She also understood why. Yes, Don was working on behalf of Pinafore, but he was really doing this for her. If she had declined, he would have been disappointed, but his generosity was genuine. Just as others had helped make him successful, he was doing the same for her. She heard this same theme from Andre Durand, Will Little, Glenn Frommer, Beth McQuiston—nearly everyone she interviewed. Helping others succeed or be happy was a strong element of their success in life. And that's why on her final flight home a light bulb had gone off in her head. She had to interview Don! Of all the generous acts and people she'd learned about and from in the past six months, the most meaningful for her had been right in front of her the entire time.

That was the brilliance of the entire plan. *He helped me*, she thought, *knowing I would want to help others*. It's that crazy ripple effect that Mike Kaplan referred to and Ayman El-Mohandes mentioned about impacting students. And, Emily thought, *what a career opportunity*. Chief Generosity Officer was a title that had never existed. If Don followed through on his offer, she would have the opportunity to make it something known far and wide. Maybe she could become the inception point of some mantra that let people know 'doing good leads to doing well.' *They may write about me in books one day*, she thought. Ha!

> That was the brilliance of the entire plan. *He helped me,* she thought, *knowing I would want to help others.*

In addition to her optimism, she was admittedly a little embarrassed that she hadn't had faith in the beginning, and even pushed back thinking this was a ruse to make her quit. Looking back, she realized she'd actually made a lot of assumptions, likely out of fear. But that didn't excuse her attitude. By accepting this challenge she'd grown in her thinking, in her patience, and certainly in her faith that doing good leads to more good.

Emily had almost a week before her meeting with Don, and she was determined to use that time as efficiently as possible. She spent her first day home setting up a workstation in the living area, adding a couple small succulents to the windowsills so she could have a little company for the big project she was about to undertake.

Chris Graves had sent her a comprehensive accumulation of studies, and Andre had made some AI suggestions. She wanted to combine those with all her interview notes and previous research and turn them into something—a tool, a resource, a plan, something to inspire others to want to learn about the power of generosity. Nobody had a clear formula; many had shared valuable ideas, examples, and concepts. Now, it was up to her to pull it all together.

She had a moment of hesitation, then remembered Andy Hill saying that generosity takes courage and Sherrie Beckstead that generosity takes confidence. Yep, she would need to take some risks. If she really wanted to make a difference, she would need to convey something that many seemed to vaguely understand but not practice with intention, let alone with a plan. It was okay because she had okay-ness. She knew what she wanted to do was based on authentic generosity.

So, let's start at the beginning, she thought and pulled out the VMVP (vision, mission, values, passion) Don had her read when they'd last met. Her passion for travel hadn't changed, and her vision to be known as a leader and a visionary was consistent. Her values still made her proud. She felt like she was really getting back to the person who wrote those. But her mission had changed. Yes, service to others was still important, but she had no intention of limiting that service to people who were visiting a hotel. She would expand her mission statement to include learning from the stories and experiences of others. She would also include a direct reference to generosity and how she would learn, deploy, and teach this amazingly powerful way of life. She was destined for this.

Okay, now back to the plan. She needed something in writing to share with Don. He knew she wanted the job. He was not going to deny her, no way. But she wanted to prove to him that what he had done was wise. He didn't expect anything in return, but she wanted him to feel great about his decision.

It might have taken her twelve interviews and six months, but she was determined to show Don that she understood the assignment. It didn't matter what religion someone practiced, what family dynamic they had, or even if they'd been exposed to generosity in the past; every human had a unique, innate ability to be generous and to use that power to drive their success.

Emily pulled out her computer and began to write. The first words were easy:

Inspiring Generosity – Training Plan

There was a lot to incorporate. So she began with the history of generosity.

The fact that broad generosity was truly unique to humans was standout in her mind. Research shows that only humans are generous with others outside of their families or communities, with those whom they don't know. Beth had said this was a big contributor to the evolution of human society. Of course it was. Generosity leads to trust, trust leads to relationship, and relationships lead to community. We are literally hardwired to be helpful to others, for the sake of our continued existence. Emily thought about the careers and choices that some people make, like joining the military. Those choices are not only courageous but also incredibly generous and focused on the greater good. She was a bit surprised that Don hadn't suggested interviewing a veteran. *Oh well*, she thought, *I guess he can't think of everything.*

She went back to the Internet and typed in "generosity and health" and "generosity and healing." She wasn't surprised by anything but was astounded by the volume of research on how acts of generosity help people heal mentally, emotionally, and even physically. *Superpower* was the term that kept coming to her.

Her space was covered in sticky notes and piles of printed paper. Amused, she thought that Glenn would approve.

Next, Emily took Andre's advice and tried her hand at artificial intelligence. ChatGPT was one of the first AI platforms, and she was curious what it would have to say. She typed: Describe the power of generosity.

The response darted up instantaneously:

The power of generosity lies in its ability to create positive ripple effects that can transform individuals, communities, and even the world at large. When we give freely of our time, resources, or talents, we not only help those in need but also inspire others to do the same.

Generosity is a powerful force that can create a sense of abundance, joy, and gratitude in both the giver and the receiver. It can foster stronger relationships, build trust, and create a sense of connection among people from different backgrounds and cultures.

Moreover, generosity can also have significant health benefits. Studies have shown that giving can reduce stress, lower blood pressure, and even increase lifespan.

Generosity can also have an impact on society as a whole. When we give to charitable organizations or support causes we care about, we can help address social and environmental issues and create a more equitable and sustainable world.

Overall, the power of generosity lies in its ability to create positive change and transform both individuals and society. By cultivating a spirit of generosity, we can build stronger relationships, create a sense of connection and purpose, and make a meaningful impact on the world around us.

> "Overall, the power of generosity lies in its ability to create positive change and transform both individuals and society."

Emily paused for a moment, absorbing all the information that AI had just dropped in her lap. The words were so powerful. Amazingly they validated nearly everything she had learned in the interviews. They missed the rich texture of the stories, but the same messages came through. She remembered an article from a magazine on the plane. AI scans all of the known data in the world, some 64 zettabytes (a trillion gigabytes), and creates responses. What a powerful validation! Again, *superpower* came to mind. *Darn you, Don,* she laughed.

She was on a roll. Emily's fingers tapped once more, posing the question buzzing through her brain: Describe the science behind the power of generosity?

ChatGPT again responded immediately:

There is a growing body of scientific research that supports the idea that generosity can have a profound impact on our physical and emotional well-being as well as on our relationships and the world around us.

One of the key mechanisms behind the power of generosity is the release of feel-good neurotransmitters such as dopamine and oxytocin in the brain. When we give or receive something, these neurotransmitters are released, which can create feelings of happiness, connection, and satisfaction.

Research has also shown that generosity can reduce stress and promote physical health. A study published in the *Journal of Health Psychology* found that people who volunteered regularly had lower levels of the stress hormone cortisol as well as lower blood pressure and a lower risk of heart disease.

Generosity can also have a positive impact on our relationships. A study published in the *Journal of Social Psychology* found that couples who reported higher levels of generosity toward each other were more satisfied with their relationship and less likely to experience conflict.

Moreover, generosity can have a ripple effect, inspiring others to give and creating a culture of giving within communities. A study published in the journal *Nature Communications* found that when people saw others engaging in acts of kindness and generosity, they were more likely to do the same.

Overall, the science behind the power of generosity suggests that giving can have a significant impact on our physical and emotional well-being, our relationships, and the world around us. By cultivating a spirit of generosity, we can improve our own lives and contribute to a more compassionate and connected world.

Emily again thought about the incredible list of studies Chris had shared with her. Everyone should see that list; everyone should have access to those studies and all of the incredible findings. Chris said I could share it, so that is what I'm going to do.

Okay, one more question for ChatGPT:

List the many forms of generosity.

The program waited a moment, then the answer came in ten succinct points:

Generosity can take many different forms, some of which include:

1. Financial generosity: giving money or material possessions to others.
2. Time generosity: donating one's time or energy to help others, whether through volunteering, mentoring, or simply being present for someone who needs support.
3. Emotional generosity: offering emotional support, empathy, and understanding to others.
4. Forgiveness: letting go of grudges or resentment and extending grace to those who have wronged us.
5. Hospitality: welcoming others into our homes, our lives, and our hearts.
6. Charitable giving: donating to charitable organizations or causes that we believe in.
7. Kindness: small acts of kindness, like holding the door for someone or offering a smile to a stranger.

8. Listening: truly listening to others and showing interest in their lives and concerns.
9. Thoughtfulness: anticipating the needs of others and going out of our way to help or support them.
10. Encouragement: providing motivation, inspiration, and encouragement to others to help them achieve their goals or overcome obstacles.

Hmm, it's a pretty good list, but AI's not perfect. I think there are many more forms. I'll figure that out later.

It all ties together, she thought. Don had asked her to read *The Good Life,* a book that summarized a Harvard study, the largest and longest study ever done on happiness. The conclusions were essentially that healthy relationships lead to a happy life. We now know that "generosity leads to trust and trusting interactions, and thus contributes significantly to healthy relationships." Don obviously knew that all along. What the Harvard people knew, but didn't call out specifically, was how important generosity was in the process.

It's all here, but a bit overwhelming. Time to simplify and create a plan outline:

Inspiring Generosity – Training Plan

Summary of Findings:
1. Interviews:
   - Twelve interviews.
   - All shared unique and powerful perspectives on generosity.
   - In every case all agreed generosity led to personal happiness and success.
2. Science:

- The abundant science on the power of generosity is indisputable.
- Beth shared numerous studies about evolution and survival.
- Chris's list will be incorporated into the sharing.

3. Uniquely Human:
   - Major point of credibility to incorporate. Eye-opening and so powerful.
   - Broad generosity (with unknown others) is uniquely human.
   - Generosity is accredited with helping to enable the evolution of society.

4. Technology:
   - AI searches validate all findings.
   - Technology could be used to accelerate generosity if people better understood its power.
   - Social platforms magnify or accelerate karma. There is no place to hide.

5. Relationships and Trust:
   - The HBR study.
   - Research—generosity fuels trust.
   - Research—generosity fuels healthy relationships.

6. The Ripple Effect:
   - The more you do, the more you want to do.
   - Encourages the recipient to be generous.
   - Encourages others that witness the act to be generous (role model).

7. Self-generosity:
   - Enables one to be more generous with others.
   - Ties to VMVP in terms of being authentic and consistent.

- The difference between self-generosity and overindulgence.
- Acknowledges the physical and mental benefits of generosity (hormones).
- Acknowledges the probability of karma.

Next steps:
1. Define generosity so others can better understand what it is.
2. Somehow summarize what is stated above so people can understand that the power is *real*.
3. Inspire people to be generous or to become more generous and thus reap the benefits of generosity.
4. Help others understand how to effectively incorporate generosity into their daily lives.
5. Help others align their VMVP with generosity in ways that are authentic to them.
6. Help others prioritize when, where, and how to best be generous in ways that are authentic to them.
7. Demonstrate ways to dramatically scale generosity for maximum impact and benefit.

Okay, I have a lot to do. No wonder this hasn't been done before. No wonder Don has created an entirely new role. Ha—no wonder he picked me. He knew I would be passionate enough to take on the challenge. Don likes one-page plans. I'll get this formatted the way he likes it and hand it to him during our meeting.

Emily smiled to herself, thinking of all the benefits of generosity and the science behind it. She had learned so much in the last six months. She thought of the good she could do by consciously increasing her generosity and teaching others to do the same. *The possibilities are endless*, she reflected, *for me, for others, and quite frankly for Pinafore.*

Well, today was the last day of this portion of her journey. Time for some reflection and self-generosity. She headed out for a stroll and to soak up the last bit of sun for the day.

CHAPTER 18

DON'S DECISION

Alot had transpired since Emily had last seen Don. Her memories of being disappointed and scared, and also suspicious and apprehensive, were all still very vivid. Though it seemed like yesterday, it also seemed like years ago. The travel, the interviews, the research, the time to think, and some time for much-needed self-generosity made the last six months feel like a lifetime of learning.

Before she knew it Emily was landing at DFW. She had flown into Dallas many times. Though it was a monstrous airport, the design was brilliant, with luggage retrieval and transportation within steps from every gate. She didn't have checked bags, so she walked right by the carousel and opened her Uber app. Twenty-three minutes to Legacy West. Perfect.

When she jumped out of the car, Emily had a curious question in her head. She felt like she should hug Don when she saw him. She had never hugged him before. She hadn't been the hugging type, but now somehow it felt appropriate.

Before she had even gotten to the door Don appeared and the two hugged. It was very natural and genuine, yet completely professional. She almost laughed.

"Hello," Don said, smiling from ear to ear. Emily was sure it was a proud father's smile.

"Hi Don," she replied with a matching smile. "Are you ready to be interviewed? I'm pretty good at this now, you know."

Don had reserved a gorgeous conference room on the thirty-first floor, with floor-to-ceiling glass windows that looked over the expanse of North Texas. No majestic mountains, but the land was dotted with beautiful buildings and gorgeous green campuses. All the papers talked about companies moving to Texas and hordes of people following. *The land of opportunity*, Emily thought to herself, much like Silicon Valley fifty years ago.

Emily mentioned how complimentary people had been of Don. That led to a good thirty minutes of conversation about all the people she had met. They laughed and both shared stories, until Emily mentioned Jack Pannell had talked about some trouble the two had been in. "Care to tell me more?" Emily asked with a twinkle in her eyes.

With the poise of a veteran politician, Don ignored the comment and said, "So Emily, I understand you want to interview me, let's get started. I don't have all day."

She knew he was playing, but also serious. "If you insist," she said, grinning at Don as she asked her first question.

"I probably know more about generosity then anyone on the planet, but still feel like there is a lot to learn. Everyone I talked with had such unique experiences and ideas. But everyone agreed on one thing: If you are generous with others, with no expectation of exchange or return, it will lead you to eudemonic success. Is that what you sent me out to learn?"

Don raised a brow. "One of my favorite words," he said. "Happiness gained through actualization or achievement of purpose is by far the most rewarding. Yes, I believe that generosity is the superpower that enables eudemonic well-being, or happiness. When we first met and I asked you to write your vision, mission, values, and passion, it was all about understanding if you were purpose driven. You clearly were and still are. Helping others, being of service or service leadership, as Andre always talks about, is the most powerful way to make it happen. Positive karma is assured. So, yes, that is part of what I was hoping you would learn."

Emily nodded. "Vision, mission, values, and passion were all things many brought up either explicitly or in their own way," she said. "Melissa Dawn Simkins has actually made a career helping people develop their MVP (Mission, Vision, Purpose), and Chris Graves shared so much about understanding who people really are and their motivations. So it's clear that doing this work provides intentional focus. But how exactly does it tie to being generous or harnessing the power of generosity?"

"In many ways." Don had become serious. "This is a great question and really demonstrates what you have learned. Without understanding who you want to be and your mission and values, it's very difficult to know how you can best be generous. When you help people in ways that directly align with elements of your VMVP, then being generous is more effective and authentic. It aligns your generous acts with the person you want to become. There are millions of ways to be generous and millions of opportunities. If you have a well-defined VMVP, then your decisions on how you can be uniquely generous at any given time will be better. Does that make sense?"

> "When you help people in ways that directly align with elements of your VMVP, then being generous is more effective and authentic."

"Perfect sense," Emily said. "I think it was Leigh Steinberg who talked about how each moment is an opportunity to make a choice that demonstrates your values."

Don continued, "Exactly. I know you learned a lot about self-generosity. Some of the people you met are good at it, some maybe not so much. Self-care is about giving yourself—your mind, your body, and your spirit—what you need to become who you want to be. This is so important. Self-generosity is not self-indulgence; it's also not living with scarcity. It's about being in touch with what you need now, to be more generous with everyone, longer. If you are in poor physical, mental, or spiritual health, you can't serve others optimally. I'm sure Sherrie helped you understand that. There's a woman who gave of herself to others until the well came close to dry. On the other hand, as I'm sure you heard from Will Little, serving others is a great way to heal or help yourself. The key is simply understanding who you are. I wish more people did. I hope more of our employees will soon." And he smiled.

"I'm a bit in awe of all the positive aspects of generosity," Emily said. "Just the studies I received from Chris Graves and the science learned from Beth McQuiston were mind-boggling. It's really cut-and-dry, true generosity improves the well-being of the giver—again, if given with no expectation of return from the recipient. Then you take into account the effect generosity has on the recipient, then the ripple or compounding effect when the recipient passes it on to others. What am I missing?"

"Two important things," Don said after a moment to think. "First, often a person's generosity is witnessed by others. That example motivates others to do more of the same. I've seen studies that detail this and see it at our hotels all the time. That compounding effect you mentioned is bigger than just the ripples from the recipient. Second, you used the word *karma*. That positive energy you put out into the world, some call it love, inevitably *will* come back to you. We all know it. Why people don't embrace this wisdom is beyond me."

"And that thinking, expecting karma to benefit you, isn't being selfish?" Emily questioned, knowing the answer but wanting to hear it from Don, as it would be an important element of her training.

Don was smiling again. "Absolutely not," he said. "A wise person knows that living a life of generosity or service is always rewarded, usually in unexpected and abundant ways. If that understanding is combined with a clear VMVP, then it will happen faster and even more abundantly."

"Thank you, Don. This stuff is so powerful. I don't want to get too personal, but can you tell me where you learned about generosity? Was it from your parents, your grandparents?" Emily asked.

"No one person," Don said. "Many people have inspired me. I grew up in a lower-middle-class family. My dad taught me a lot about what happens when you are not generous. He was a valuable role model, but not in a good way. My mom is perhaps the kindest, most generous person I know. She was the top salesperson in Walla Walla, Washington, for many years. She's retired now, but she really knew how to *see* people. She remembers everyone's name. She always remembered what they shared with her about their lives. She cared about her clients and would never sell them something that wasn't right. Most importantly, she made people feel important. She enhanced their lives. I watched her do this for much of my life. It was such a blessing.

"Mike Hinkle was a very close friend of mine. In high school, he was the handsome guy, with the cool car, and was an incredible athlete. That was not me in high school. Ha. He was also two years older than I was. But Mike was humble and empathetic. He took an interest in me. I was only sixteen, but he had me thinking about my vision in life. He shared the power God plays in his life. And, he constantly talked about being generous with your spirit. Every day he would try to find someone in a bad mood so that he could tackle the challenge of making them smile. He probably would have been an ideal client for Leigh had he pursued a career in sports. Mike and I were close for many years. He passed recently of a brain aneurysm. Him gone leaves a big hole in my life. Do you want more?"

"If you are willing," Emily said.

"Mike taught me to seek out wise people to learn from," Don continued. "I took Dale Carnegie classes, I bought some of the very first cassette tapes published by Tony Robbins. I'm sure that ages me, but the tapes were amazing. They gave me a formula built around being of service to others. I still follow and listen to Robbins. I also love listening to the Ed Mylett podcast. He interviews inspirational people, the best and the brightest in various endeavors. Many of his podcast guests talk about generosity and relationships. I've read books and listened to YouTube videos by Malala, Brené Brown, the list goes on and on. I won't bore you with more. I'll give you a list of resources that I lean on to continue learning and growing if it's helpful."

"That would be tremendous. Perhaps I can share the list with the teams?" she asked.

"Of course," Don said.

"I feel like I'm breaking new ground with this training," Emily continued with a smile, "if you give me the position, that is. The next challenge is that not everyone will have the privilege of meeting the people you so generously introduced me to. So how do we teach them—no, how do I *inspire* them—to want to learn about the power of generosity? How can they understand what a tremendous impact it can have on their life and the lives of so many others?"

Don looked at Emily intently. "My goal was to inspire you. I knew that if I did, you would figure out how to inspire others. I'm confident you will figure it out. Are you as confident?"

Emily smiled. "You know I love a challenge. The fact that what you are asking for has never been done before invigorates me. The idea of inspiring others excites me. Sure, it's scary, but I'm okay with that. It's not about controlling the outcome; it's about creating the opportunity."

Don nodded kindly. "So, I have something for you before you go," he said, rising and walking across the room to a conspicuous box sitting on the end of the conference room table. He handed it to Emily.

Emily opened it and stared at her new business cards:

Emily Gardner
Chief Generosity Officer
Pinafore Global

"Thank you," she said after a moment, feeling all of the emotions anyone can experience at one time.

"That's not a gift," Don said. "You earned those cards. You represented Pinafore beautifully on your journey and you learned everything you needed to learn."

This time, there was no thinking: Emily jumped up and gave Don a hug. "I won't let you down. I won't let *them* down," she said, referring to the global team members she would be meeting soon. "Oh, I know you like brief one-page plans; here is mine. I look forward to your thoughts and suggestions."

They were together for about an hour and a half. As Emily walked out the door, she realized she was emotionally spent but too excited to slow down. She went directly to the Starbucks down the street, ordered her latte, pulled out the Inspiration Planner she'd been given by Melissa, and began to add the details and incorporate what Don had shared. There was still so much she wanted to be able to share with others.

For a moment, she silently marveled on Don's generosity, then realized he was probably feeling great right now. *I'll bet his endorphins are spiking*, she thought, then laughed out loud.

When the barista walked out from behind the counter to hand her the latte, Emily looked her straight in the eyes, thanked her, then with sincere interest asked, "How long have you been a barista?" The young woman smiled, and they chatted a bit, then she hustled back to work.

Yep, that felt good, Emily said to herself.

This is going to be fun!

UNLEASHING YOUR SUPERPOWER:
A WORD FROM THE AUTHORS

We would like to thank you for joining Emily on her epic journey to better understand the power of generosity. We hope you enjoyed it as much as we did.

We would also like to thank our interviewed contributors. Their unique personal experiences, fabulous insights, and remarkable wisdom are gifts to us all. A huge thank you!

Though the interviews highlighted many important elements of generosity, two very important concepts stand out.

1) Generosity is any act of kindness or support given with no expectation of exchange or return from the recipient. There are limitless, meaningful, powerful ways to be generous.

2) Knowing you are benefiting yourself by being generous with others is NOT being selfish. It is being wise. If you don't expect a return from the recipient, but you know you benefit physically, mentally, emotionally, and abundantly in the long term, then you understand the true power of generosity.

Comprehending these two things enables endless opportunities for everyone to be generous every day and ignites a superpower that benefits both the recipient and giver. Generosity Wins means generosity wins for all. Generosity is a win/win.

So why do we need to radically redefine generosity? Why do we need to make generosity more meaningful and available to everyone? Why now?

The challenges mankind faces today, and will face tomorrow, are as daunting as they are abundant. Yet the opportunities are just as abundant. How we respond will determine whether we thrive or struggle. Humanity has advanced based on our ability to form communities, relationships, and vast governing bodies. We are the only known living creature that strives to be generous with others we don't know and may never know. This unique attribute has sustained and propelled our development over the ages. We will thrive if we build on this unique attribute.

> **Humans are the only known living creature that strives to be generous with others we don't know and may never know.**

It won't be easy, of course. As we are all very aware, humankind faces a myriad of crises. For example, the US Surgeon General declared in May of 2023 that we have a loneliness crisis in our country, a crisis propelled by the Covid pandemic and exacerbated by the misuse of technology. Add this to the suicide crisis, the growing emotional-health crisis, and many others that plague humankind today, and the seas we must sail look anything but smooth.

As an added complication, media outlets of every type continue to publish articles on the potential hazards that artificial intelligence could bring to our lives. Will there be challenges? Probably. Will there be benefits? Very likely. Will artificial intelligence be *generous*? Not likely. We asked ChatGPT the question, "Is, or can, AI be generous?" The immediate answer was that AI does not possess emotions or intentions, including generosity. AI is a computational system designed to process information and perform tasks based on algorithms. Once again, what is uniquely human will undoubtedly continue to be our strategic advantage propelling our strength, growth, and advancement, *if* we embrace it.

Each of us can play a role in reversing the downward spiral we read about daily. It will require collaboration, and it will require generosity.

Many believe kindness can change the world, or understanding, or empathy, or sharing. We believe all are correct. But the power of these actions is amplified exponentially when done with no expectation of exchange or return from those being helped. When done with generosity, versus with an agenda, all these acts have the power to change lives and enhance the world.

Is generosity a tool, a behavior, a way of living, a way of being, a magical power, a spiritual power? *Yes* to all the above! Our human tendency to be generous, to help others, inevitably helps ourselves. We all thirst for purpose. Our happiness is dependent on having and proceeding toward a purpose. What we now understand is that generosity enhances emotional well-being, contributes to abundance, and also provides a road map for purpose.

We sit on the precipice. Will we succumb to fear, division, and blame, or rely on our uniquely human instincts to overcome by rebuilding trust, relationships, and community? Powerful forces are pushing us apart. These forces are fueled by greed and control. We can mitigate these destructive forces with generosity.

The more we researched generosity, the more we realized there was to learn. The science is abundant. Please take time to follow the QR code in the Resources section to the studies we've provided. Learn more about:

- The direct benefits of teaching children the power of generosity.
- Ways to stem teenage suicides. The science shows teens are missing the connections that make life meaningful.
- Keys to empowering young adults, showing them they can be generous *and* be successful—that one leads to the other.
- The importance of role models. Regardless of age, stage, or status in life, the world needs role models. Studies show seeing generosity in action motives others to be generous.

We endorse generosity because it is a singular powerful focus. It is core to who and what it means to be human. It is a component of relationships, of community, of organizational and spiritual beliefs. It's simple, not "seven steps to the good life" or "ten keys to abundance." *One* focus! One simple thing to remember, think about, and act on every day. One powerful tool.

> **We endorse generosity because it is core to who and what it means to be human.**

This book is an introduction, or awakening, to the superpower, but there are many forms, applications, and implications of generosity. Mastering the superpower is the next challenge.

How does one become generous; what's the easiest way?

How does one maximize generosity?

How does one scale generosity for optimal impact and benefit?

How does one prioritize generosity?

How does one effectively be self-generous?

How does one inspire others with generosity?

How will generosity shift the tilt of the world?

We hope to provide more information and guidance soon. In the meantime, our challenge to you is to perform one act of generosity a day. One kindness, one sharing, one mentoring, with no expectation of exchange or return from whom you are helping. Journal your actions every day for thirty days. Monitor how it feels. Observe the effects on your mental and physical health. Monitor how your life begins to change. Start today—you may be surprised how impactful it will be.

If you've found this book to be insightful or beneficial, we encourage you to pass it on, or gift a copy to someone who could benefit. Maybe a teacher, a family member, a co-worker, or just a friend. You might even choose someone randomly. You are human.

Give your children, family, friends, and co-workers the wisdom to leverage this superpower. You will not regret it.

Warmly,

Monte and Nicole

GENEROSITY WINS

Resources & References

The following QR code provides direct links to documents, forms, and other reference materials for your exclusive use. Just scan the code to access and download.

*

Vision / Mission / Values / Passion (VMVP)
Directions and forms to guide you in creating your own VMVP
Become exactly who you want to be.
Fun and easy to complete.

*

Self-Generosity
Comprehensive overview, tools, and forms
Understand what self-generosity is and
how to make it a life-changing practice.

*

The Science of Generosity
Links to studies on the power of generosity.

*

People, Podcasts, Books, and Etcetera
A compilation of resources we referenced in the book and
others we feel may be of value to you on your journey.

*

Buy copies of this book to give as gifts
We'll take care of all the details and include
a beautiful, personalized gift card.